Top 100 Most Delicious

Empanada Recipes

An Empanada Cookbook

by Graham Bourdain

Copyright © 2023 Graham Bourdain

All Rights Reserved

Disclaimer

Reasonable care has been taken to ensure that the information presented in this ebook is accurate. However, the reader should understand that the information provided does not constitute legal, medical or professional advice of any kind.

No Liability: this product is supplied "as is" and without warranties. All warranties, express or implied, are hereby disclaimed. Use of this product constitutes acceptance of the "No Liability" policy. If you do not agree with this policy, you are not permitted to use or distribute this product.

We shall not be liable for any losses or damages whatsoever

(including, without limitation, consequential loss or damage) directly or indirectly arising from the use of this product.

Please note that the nutritional values may vary depending on the specific ingredients and measurements used, as well as the method of cooking.

It's always a good idea to consult a registered dietitian or use an online nutrition calculator to get the most accurate nutritional value for a recipe, based on the ingredients and measurements you use.

Table of Contents

Pork

Turkey

Tuna

Seafood

<u>Vegetable etc.</u>

Egg

Other

Bonus recipes for empanada dough

Review Request

1. Beef and Potato Empanadas

Prep: 15 min. Cook: 30 min. Ready in: 45 min. Servings: 6

Ingredients:

1 lb. beef, diced

2 medium potatoes, peeled and diced

1 onion, diced

2 cloves of garlic, minced

1 tsp paprika

1 tsp cumin

Salt and pepper to taste

4 tbsp of cilantro, chopped

4 tbsp of raisins (optional)

1 package of empanada dough (store-bought or homemade)

1 egg, beaten (for egg wash)

Cooking Directions:

Alright folks, listen up. This recipe is a classic and it's going to knock your socks off. Beef and Potato Empanadas, it's a combination of flavors that just can't be beat.

Let's start with the filling. Take a pan, throw in some diced beef, and brown it up real nice. Drain off any excess fat and add in some diced onions and minced garlic. Give it a good stir and let those onions sweat and caramelize. Now, add in some diced potatoes, it will bring a nice texture to this dish. Season that with some paprika, cumin, salt, and pepper, and you're on your way to flavor town.

Add in some raisins, if you like, it will give a nice contrast of sweet and savory. Remove from heat and let it cool down before you start assembling your empanadas.

Next, roll out your empanada dough. I like mine to be about 1/8 inch thick. Cut out some circles. Place a tablespoon of filling on one side of the dough circle. Brush the edges of the dough with the beaten egg. Fold the dough over the filling, forming a half-moon shape and press the edges to seal. Brush the top with the beaten egg. Place the empanadas on a baking sheet lined with parchment paper.

Pop those bad boys in the oven at 375F (190C) for 20-25 minutes or until golden brown. Serve 'em up nice and warm, maybe with some chimichurri or aji on the side.

And there you have it, folks. The perfect beef and potato empanadas. Savor it, and don't be shy with the hot sauce.

Enjoy

2. Beef and Onion Empanadas

Prep: 20 min. Cook: 20 min. Ready In: 40 min. Servings: 4

Ingredients:

1 pound ground beef

1/2 cup diced onion

1/4 teaspoon cumin

1/4 teaspoon smoked paprika

1/4 teaspoon black pepper

1/4 teaspoon salt

1/4 cup grated cheddar cheese

1/4 cup grated Monterey Jack cheese

1 package (15 oz) store-bought empanada dough

1 large egg, beaten with 1 tablespoon water

Cooking Directions:

Alright folks, get ready for a delicious treat with these Beef and Onion Empanadas.

First things first, preheat your oven to 375 degrees F. Next, heat a skillet over medium-high heat and cook the beef until browned, about 5 minutes. Remove the beef from the skillet with a slotted spoon and set it aside. Add the diced onion to the skillet, and cook until softened, about 5 minutes. Stir in the cumin, smoked paprika, black pepper, and salt. Cook for another minute. Stir in the beef, cheddar cheese and Monterey Jack cheese into the skillet, cook until cheese melted.

Now it's time to assemble the empanadas. Roll out the empanada dough on a lightly floured surface to about 1/8-inch thickness. Cut the dough into 4-inch circles using a round cookie cutter or the rim of a glass.

Spoon about 2 tablespoons of the beef and onion filling onto one half of each dough circle, leaving a 1/2-inch border around the edges. Brush the beaten egg around the edges of the dough, then fold the dough over the filling to form a half-moon shape. Press the edges together to seal.

Place the empanadas on a baking sheet and brush the tops with the remaining beaten egg. Bake for 20 minutes, or until golden brown.

Serve hot, garnished with fresh chopped parsley, or with a spicy salsa on the side. And don't forget a cold beer because these empanadas are going to be a hit.

Enjoy

3. Beef and Mushroom Empanadas

Prep: 15 min. Cook: 20 min. Ready in: 35 min. Servings: 8

Ingredients:

1 lb. ground beef

1/2 onion, diced

1/2 cup diced mushrooms

1/4 cup chopped fresh parsley

1/4 cup raisins

1/4 cup chopped green olives

1/4 cup diced green bell pepper

2 cloves garlic, minced

2 tablespoons tomato paste

1 teaspoon ground cumin

1/2 teaspoon salt

1/4 teaspoon black pepper

2 tablespoons olive oil

1 egg, beaten

store-bought empanada dough

Cooking Directions:

Listen, folks, you wanna make some empanadas that'll knock the socks off your friends and family? You gotta start with the filling, and let me tell you, this beef and mushroom mixture is a real winner.

First, heat a large skillet over medium-high heat and add the olive oil. Once that oil is hot, toss in the onions, garlic, bell pepper and mushrooms. Cook until softened, about 5 minutes. Add the ground beef, cumin, salt, and pepper. Cook until the beef is browned, about 5-7 minutes. Now, you're going to add in the raisins, olives, parsley, and tomato paste. Cook for another 2-3 minutes, stirring frequently. You want all those flavors to meld together, to create a filling that's going to make your taste buds dance. Once that filling is done, take it off the heat and let it cool. This is important, because if you try to put hot filling in your empanadas, it's going to make a mess of your dough. Trust me, I've made that mistake before. Now, preheat your oven to 375F.

Take your store-bought empanada dough, roll it out, and cut it into circles. Place a spoonful of the beef and mushroom mixture in the center of each circle. Brush the edges with the beaten egg, and then fold the dough over, pressing the edges to seal.

Place the empanadas on a baking sheet and brush the tops with the remaining beaten egg. Bake for 20 minutes or until golden brown.

And there you have it folks, Beef and Mushroom Empanadas that are going to make you the star of the show. Pair it with a cold beer and enjoy the ride, you deserve it.

Enjoy

4. Beef and Bell Pepper Empanadas

Prep: 30 min. Cook: 20 min. Ready in: 50 min. Servings: 4

Ingredients:

1 tablespoon olive oil

1/2 cup diced onion

1 pound ground beef

1 cup diced red or green bell pepper

1/2 teaspoon dried thyme

1/2 teaspoon salt

1/4 teaspoon black pepper

1 package of empanada dough

1 egg, beaten

Cooking Directions:

Gather 'round, all you foodies and empanada enthusiasts! Today, we're whipping up a delicious dish of juicy beef and sweet bell peppers, all nestled inside a flaky, golden crust.

To start, heat the olive oil in a large skillet over medium heat. Add the onion and cook until soft and translucent, about 5 minutes. Then, add the ground beef and cook until browned, about 7-10 minutes. Stir in the diced bell peppers, thyme, salt, and pepper, and cook for another 2-3 minutes. Set aside to cool.

Next, preheat your oven to 375°F and line a baking sheet with parchment paper. Roll out the empanada dough on a lightly floured surface to 1/8-inch thickness. Cut the dough into 4-inch rounds. Spoon about 2 tablespoons of the beef and bell pepper filling onto one half of each round, leaving a 1/2-inch border around the edges. Brush the edges with the beaten egg and fold the other half of the dough over the filling, pressing the edges to seal. Place the empanadas on the prepared baking sheet and brush the tops with the remaining egg.

Bake the empanadas for 20-25 minutes, or until they're golden brown and crispy.

And there you have it, the perfect empanada for a satisfying meal. Each flaky bite is packed with juicy beef and sweet bell peppers, making for a delicious and savory experience. So go ahead, grab a bite and enjoy the flavors of this Latin-inspired dish.

Enjoy

5. Beef and Blue Cheese Empanadas

Prep: 20 min. Cook: 20 min. Ready In: 40 min. Servings: 4

Ingredients:

1 pound ground beef

1/2 cup diced onion

1/2 cup diced red bell pepper

1/4 cup diced jalapeno pepper

1/4 cup diced poblano pepper

1/4 cup diced green bell pepper

1/2 teaspoon ground cumin

1/2 teaspoon smoked paprika

1/4 teaspoon cayenne pepper

1/4 teaspoon black pepper

1/4 teaspoon salt

1/4 cup crumbled blue cheese

1/4 cup grated cheddar cheese

1/4 cup grated Monterey Jack cheese

1 package (15 oz) store-bought empanada dough

1 large egg, beaten with 1 tablespoon water

Cooking Directions:

Get ready for a flavorful explosion with these Beef and Blue Cheese Empanadas. The perfect combination of savory beef and tangy blue cheese in a flaky crust. Let's get cooking!

First things first, preheat your oven to 375 degrees F. Next, heat a skillet over medium-high heat and cook the beef until browned, about 5 minutes. Remove the beef from the skillet with a slotted spoon and set it aside. Add the onion, red bell pepper, jalapeno pepper, poblano pepper, and green bell pepper to the skillet, and cook until softened, about 5 minutes. Stir in the cumin, smoked paprika, cayenne pepper, black pepper, and salt. Cook for another minute. Stir in the crumbled blue cheese, cheddar cheese and Monterey Jack cheese into the beef mixture, cook until cheese melted. Now it's time to assemble the empanadas. Roll out the empanada dough on a lightly floured surface to about 1/8-inch thickness. Cut the dough into 4-inch circles using a round cookie cutter or the rim of a glass. Spoon about 2 tablespoons of the beef and blue cheese filling onto one half of each dough circle, leaving a 1/2-inch border around the edges. Brush the beaten egg around the edges of the dough, then fold the dough over the filling to form a half-moon shape. Press the edges together to seal. Place the empanadas on a baking sheet and brush the tops with the remaining beaten egg. Bake for 20 minutes, or until golden brown. Serve hot, garnished with fresh chopped parsley, or with a spicy salsa on the side. And don't forget a cold beer because these empanadas are going to be a hit.

Enjoy

6. Beef and Broccoli Empanadas

Prep: 30 min. Cook: 20 min. Ready in: 50 min. Servings: 4

Ingredients:

1 1/2 cups cooked and diced beef

1 cup cooked broccoli florets, diced

1/2 cup diced onion

1 clove of garlic, minced

1/2 teaspoon dried thyme

1/2 teaspoon salt

1/4 teaspoon black pepper

1 tablespoon olive oil

1 package of empanada dough

1 egg, beaten

Cooking Directions:

Get ready to sink your teeth into something delicious! Today, we're combining the savory flavors of beef and broccoli into one flaky and golden crust. These Beef and Broccoli Empanadas are sure to be a hit at your next meal.

To start, heat the olive oil in a large skillet over medium heat. Add the onion and cook until soft and translucent, about 5 minutes. Then, add the minced garlic and cook for another minute. Add the diced beef and cook for another 2-3 minutes. Stir in the broccoli, thyme, salt, and pepper, and cook for another minute. Set aside to cool.

Next, preheat your oven to 375°F and line a baking sheet with parchment paper. Roll out the empanada dough on a lightly floured surface to 1/8-inch thickness. Cut the dough into 4-inch rounds. Spoon about 2 tablespoons of the beef and broccoli filling onto one half of each round, leaving a 1/2-inch border around the edges. Brush the edges with the beaten egg and fold the other half of the dough over the filling, pressing the edges to seal. Place the empanadas on the prepared baking sheet and brush the tops with the remaining egg.

Bake the empanadas for 20-25 minutes, or until they're golden brown and crispy.

And there you have it, a delicious and savory empanada filled with the flavors of beef and broccoli. Each bite is packed with juicy and tender beef, and the crunch of broccoli. So go ahead, grab a bite and enjoy the taste of these delicious empanadas!

Enjoy

7. Beef and Green Olive Empanadas

Prep: 30 min. Cook: 20 min. Ready in: 50 min. Servings: 4

Ingredients:

1 pound ground beef

1/2 cup diced onion

1/2 cup diced green olives

1/2 teaspoon dried oregano

1/2 teaspoon ground cumin

1/2 teaspoon paprika

1/2 teaspoon salt

1/4 teaspoon black pepper

1 tablespoon olive oil

1 package of empanada dough

1 egg, beaten

Cooking Directions:

Empanadas, the perfect handheld comfort food. They're crispy, flaky, and packed with flavor. And these Beef and Green Olive Empanadas are no exception. They are the perfect way to use up any leftover ground beef you might have, and the green olives add a delicious briny twist to this classic dish.

To start, heat the olive oil in a large skillet over medium heat. Add the onion and cook until soft and translucent, about 5 minutes. Then, add the ground beef and cook until browned, about 7-8 minutes. Stir in the green olives, oregano, cumin, paprika, salt, and pepper, and cook for another 2-3 minutes. Set aside to cool.

Next, preheat your oven to 375°F and line a baking sheet with parchment paper. Roll out the empanada dough on a lightly floured surface to 1/8-inch thickness. Cut the dough into 4-inch rounds. Spoon about 2 tablespoons of the beef filling onto one half of each round, leaving a 1/2-inch border around the edges. Brush the edges with the beaten egg and fold the other half of the dough over the filling, pressing the edges to seal. Place the empanadas on the prepared baking sheet and brush the tops with the remaining egg.

Bake the empanadas for 20-25 minutes, or until they're golden brown and crispy. Serve warm and…

Enjoy

8. Beef and Guinness Empanadas

Prep: 25 min. Cook: 1h 20 min. Ready In: 1h 45 min. Servings: 4

Ingredients:

Store-bought empanada dough (12 discs)

1 lb beef chuck, cut into small cubes

1 medium onion, chopped

2 cloves garlic, minced

1 large carrot, diced

1/2 cup frozen peas

1 cup Guinness stout

1 cup beef broth

2 tablespoons tomato paste

1 tablespoon Worcestershire sauce

1 teaspoon dried thyme

1 teaspoon dried rosemary

2 tablespoons olive oil

Salt and black pepper, to taste

1 egg, beaten (for egg wash)

Cooking Directions:

Take a culinary trip to the Emerald Isle with these hearty Beef and Guinness Empanadas. Packed with tender beef, rich stout, and a medley of aromatic herbs, these empanadas are the perfect way to warm your soul on a chilly day. Whether you're celebrating St. Patrick's Day or simply craving a taste of Ireland, these empanadas are sure to hit the spot.

In a large, heavy-bottomed pot, heat the olive oil over medium heat. Add the beef cubes, season with salt and black pepper, and cook until browned on all sides. Remove the beef from the pot and set aside.

In the same pot, add the chopped onion and cook for 2 to 3 minutes, or until it begins to soften. Add the minced garlic and cook for an additional 1 minute. Stir in the diced carrot, tomato paste, Worcestershire sauce, thyme, and rosemary. Cook for about 2 minutes, allowing the flavors to meld together. Pour in the Guinness stout and beef broth, scraping up any browned bits from the bottom of the pot. Bring the mixture to a simmer. Return the browned beef to the pot and lower the heat. Cover and let it simmer for about 1 hour, or until the beef is tender. Stir in the frozen peas and cook for an additional 10 minutes. Remove from heat and let the filling cool.

Preheat your oven to 400°F (200°C) and line a baking sheet with parchment paper. Roll out the store-bought empanada dough and cut out circles about 5 inches in diameter. You can use a round cookie cutter or an appropriately sized bowl as a guide. Place a spoonful of the beef and Guinness filling in the center of each dough circle.

Fold the dough over the filling, creating a half-moon shape, and press the edges together with your fingers to seal. You can use a fork to create a decorative pattern around the edges if you'd like.

Arrange the filled empanadas on the prepared baking sheet. Brush the tops with the beaten egg to give them a gorgeous golden sheen.

Bake the empanadas for 20 to 25 minutes, or until they're golden brown and crispy. Allow them to cool for a few minutes before serving.

Enjoy

9. Beef and Carrot Empanadas

Prep: 30 min. Cook: 30 min. Ready In: 1 h. Servings: 4

Ingredients:

1 lb. beef chuck, cut into small cubes

1 onion, diced

3 cloves of garlic, minced

1 cup of grated carrots

1 teaspoon of paprika

1 teaspoon of cumin

1 teaspoon of salt

1/2 teaspoon of black pepper

1/2 teaspoon of dried oregano

1/4 cup of raisins

1/4 cup of green olives, sliced

1 package of store-bought empanada dough

1 egg, beaten

Cooking Directions:

Empanadas, my friends, are the ultimate street food. They're portable, delicious, and can be filled with just about anything. Today, we're going to show you how to make beef and carrot empanadas that will blow your mind. Trust me, these bad boys are worth the effort.

In a large skillet, brown the beef over medium-high heat until it's cooked through. Drain any excess fat. Add the onion and garlic to the skillet and cook until softened, about 5 minutes. Stir in the grated carrots, paprika, cumin, salt, black pepper, and oregano. Cook for an additional 5 minutes. Stir in the raisins and green olives and cook for a final 2 minutes. Remove from heat and let cool. Preheat the oven to 375 degrees F (190 degrees C). Roll out the store-bought empanada dough on a lightly floured surface. Cut into circles using a cookie cutter or a glass. Place a spoonful of the beef and carrot mixture on one half of each empanada dough circle. Brush the edges of the dough with the beaten egg. Fold the dough over the filling to create a half-moon shape and press the edges together to seal. Place the empanadas on a baking sheet and brush the tops with the remaining beaten egg.

Bake for 20-25 minutes, or until golden brown.

And there you have it, folks. Beef and carrot empanadas that will make your taste buds dance. Serve them up with some chimichurri or aioli and enjoy. Trust me, these are the real deal. Buen provecho!

Enjoy

10. Beef and Olive Empanadas

Prep: 15 min. Cook: 25 min. Ready in: 40 min. Servings: 4

Ingredients:

3/4 lb. ground beef

3/4 cup of green olives, chopped

1/2 onion, diced

1 1/2 cloves of garlic, minced

1/2 tsp of cumin powder

Salt and pepper to taste

3/4 package of empanada dough (store-bought or homemade)

3/4 egg, beaten (for egg wash)

Cooking Directions:

Listen up, folks. This recipe is a game-changer. Beef and Olive Empanadas, a combination of flavors that just can't be beat.

In a pan, brown the beef over medium-high heat. Add in some diced onion, minced garlic, and a teaspoon of cumin powder. Give it a good stir and let those aromatics release their flavors. Season that with some salt and pepper, and you're on your way to flavor town.

Add in some chopped green olives. Remove from heat and let it cool down before you start assembling your empanadas.

Next, roll out your empanada dough. I like mine to be about 1/8 inch thick. Cut out some circles. Place a tablespoon of filling on one side of the dough circle. Brush the edges of the dough with the beaten egg. Fold the dough over the filling, forming a half-moon shape and press the edges to seal.

Place the empanadas on a baking sheet lined with parchment paper. Brush the top with the beaten egg. Bake those bad boys in the oven at 375F (190C) for 20-25 minutes or until golden brown. Serve 'em up nice and warm, maybe with some chimichurri or aji on the side.

And there you have it folks, the perfect beef and olive empanadas.

Enjoy

11. Oven Baked Beef Empanadas

Prep: 30 min. Cook: 20 min. Ready in: 50 min. Servings: 4

Ingredients:

1 lb. salmon fillet, skin removed and cut into small cubes

1 bunch asparagus, trimmed and cut into small pieces

1 small onion, finely chopped

1 garlic clove, minced

1 tbsp olive oil

1/2 tsp cumin

1/4 tsp smoked paprika

1/4 tsp salt

1/4 tsp black pepper

1 cup shredded cheddar cheese

1 store-bought empanada dough

1 egg, beaten

Cooking Directions:

Listen up folks, it's time to elevate your empanada game.

We're going to start by prepping our fillings. Take that beautiful piece of salmon and chop it up into small cubes. Make sure to get rid of any skin, we don't need that in our empanadas. Next, take those fresh asparagus stalks and chop them up into small pieces.

In a pan, heat up some olive oil and add in the onions and garlic. Cook until the onions are translucent. Now, throw in the cumin, smoked paprika, salt, and pepper, and give it a good stir. Add in the salmon and asparagus and cook until the salmon is cooked through, and the asparagus is tender.

Take that mixture off the heat and let it cool for a bit. While that's cooling, take your store-bought dough and roll it out to about 1/8-inch thickness. Cut out circles from the dough, you should get about 8 circles. Place a spoonful of the salmon and asparagus mixture in the center of each dough circle. Top it off with a sprinkle of shredded cheddar cheese.

Now, take your beaten egg and brush the edges of each dough circle. Fold the dough in half and press the edges to seal the empanadas. Use a fork to press the edges together.

Brush the top of each empanada with the remaining beaten egg. Place the empanadas on a baking sheet lined with parchment paper and bake them in a preheated oven at 375F for 20 minutes or until the empanadas are golden brown and crispy.

Ladies and gentlemen, your Salmon and Asparagus Empanadas are ready to be devoured. These babies are the perfect balance of savory and crispy, a perfect little package of flavor. Don't be afraid to experiment with different fillings, the possibilities are endless.

Enjoy

12. Beef, Olive and Raisin Empanadas

Prep: 20 min. Cook: 25 min. Ready in: 45 min. Servings: 4

Ingredients:

Store-bought empanada dough (12 discs)

1 tablespoon olive oil

1/2 pound ground beef

1/2 cup finely chopped onion

2 garlic cloves, minced

1/2 teaspoon ground cumin

1/2 teaspoon paprika

1/4 teaspoon salt

1/4 teaspoon black pepper

1/4 cup finely chopped green olives

1/4 cup raisins

1 egg, beaten (for egg wash)

Cooking Directions:

Embark on a culinary adventure with these Beef, Olive, and Raisin Empanadas. The delightful blend of savory ground beef, tangy green olives, and sweet raisins creates a unique treat that's perfect for any mealtime occasion. Whether you serve them as a tempting appetizer or a satisfying main course, these empanadas are sure to delight.

In a large skillet, heat the olive oil over medium heat. Add the ground beef and cook, breaking it up with a spoon, for 5 to 7 minutes, or until browned and cooked through.

Add the chopped onion and minced garlic to the skillet and cook, stirring occasionally, for 3 to 5 minutes, or until the onion is softened and slightly translucent.

Stir in the ground cumin, paprika, salt, and black pepper, cooking for an additional minute.

Remove the skillet from the heat and stir in the chopped green olives and raisins, mixing well to combine.

Preheat your oven to 400°F (200°C) and line a baking sheet with parchment paper.

Roll out the store-bought empanada dough and cut out circles about 5 inches in diameter. You can use a round cookie cutter or an appropriately sized bowl as a guide.

Place a spoonful of the beef, olive, and raisin filling in the center of each dough circle.

Fold the dough over the filling, creating a half-moon shape, and press the edges together with your fingers to seal. You can use a fork to create a decorative pattern around the edges if you'd like.

Arrange the filled empanadas on the prepared baking sheet. Brush the tops with the beaten egg to give them a gorgeous golden sheen.

Bake the empanadas for 20 to 25 minutes, or until they're golden brown and crispy. Allow them to cool for a few minutes before serving.

Enjoy

13. Chicken and Corn Empanadas

Prep: 15 min. Cook: 25 min. Ready in: 40 min. Servings: 6

Ingredients:

1 lb chicken breast, diced

2 cups of sweet corn

1 onion, diced

2 cloves of garlic, minced

1 red bell pepper, diced

1/4 cup of cilantro, chopped

Salt and pepper to taste

1 package of empanada dough (store-bought or homemade)

1 egg, beaten (for egg wash)

Cooking Directions:

Let's get our hands dirty, folks. This recipe is a classic and it's going to be a crowd-pleaser. Chicken and Corn Empanadas, a combination of flavors that just can't be beat.

In a pan, brown the chicken over medium-high heat. Drain the fat. Add in some diced onions and minced garlic. Give it a good stir and let those onions sweat and caramelize. Now, add in some sweet corn, it will bring a sweet crunch to this dish. Season that with some salt and pepper, and you're on your way to flavor town. Stir in some diced red bell pepper and chopped cilantro for some extra color and flavor. Remove from heat and let it cool down before you start assembling your empanadas.

Next, roll out your empanada dough. I like mine to be about 1/8 inch thick. Cut out some circles. Place a tablespoon of filling on one side of the dough circle. Brush the edges of the dough with the beaten egg. Fold the dough over the filling, forming a half-moon shape and press the edges to seal. Brush the top with the beaten egg. Place the empanadas on a baking sheet lined with parchment paper.

Pop those bad boys in the oven at 375F (190C) for 20-25 minutes or until golden brown. Serve 'em up nice and warm, maybe with some chimichurri or aji on the side.

And there you have it folks, the perfect chicken and corn empanadas. Savor it and have fun with the toppings.

Enjoy

14. Chicken and Cheese Empanadas

Prep: 15 min. Cook: 20 min. Ready in: 35 min. Servings: 4

Ingredients:

3/4 lb. of ground chicken

3/4 cup of diced cheese (cheddar, monterey jack, or any cheese of your choice)

1/2 onion, diced

1 clove of garlic, minced

1/4 tsp of cilantro

Salt and pepper to taste

3/4 package of empanada dough (store-bought or homemade)

3/4 egg, beaten (for egg wash)

Cooking Directions:

Folks, are you ready for a cheesy twist on the classic empanada? These Chicken and Cheese Empanadas are packed with savory chicken, gooey cheese, and a hint of cilantro for an explosion of flavor in every bite. Let's get started and get our hands dirty.

Start by browning some ground chicken in a pan, add in some diced onions and minced garlic until softened. Add in some diced cheese, 1/4 tsp of cilantro, season it with some salt and pepper. Remove from heat and let it cool down before you start assembling your empanadas.

When ready, roll out your empanada dough, cut out circles and place a tablespoon of filling on one side of the dough. Brush the edges with the beaten egg, fold over, press the edges to seal. Place the empanadas on a baking sheet lined with parchment paper, brush the top with the beaten egg.

Bake in the oven at 375F (190C) for 15-20 minutes or until golden brown. Serve 'em up nice and warm, maybe with some sour cream on the side.

And there you have it folks, the perfect Chicken and Cheese Empanadas. So go ahead, indulge in the cheesy and savory flavors, and enjoy the taste of these delicious treats. Embrace the cheesy goodness and get ready to fall in love

<u>Enjoy</u>

15. Chicken and Red Pepper Empanadas

Prep: 30 min. Cook: 20 min. Ready in: 50 min. Servings: 4

Ingredients:

1 pound boneless, skinless chicken breast, cooked and diced

1 red bell pepper, diced

1/2 cup diced onion

1/2 teaspoon dried basil

1/2 teaspoon salt

1/4 teaspoon black pepper

1 tablespoon olive oil

1 package of empanada dough

1 egg, beaten

Cooking Directions:

Ladies and gentlemen, gather around for a flavor experience like no other! These Chicken and Red Pepper Empanadas are the epitome of handheld heaven, with juicy chicken and crisp red bell pepper nestled inside a flaky, golden crust. So, let's get cooking!

To start, heat the olive oil in a large skillet over medium heat. Add the onion and cook until soft and translucent, about 5 minutes. Then, add the diced chicken and red bell pepper and cook for another 2-3 minutes. Stir in the basil, salt, and pepper, and cook for another minute. Set aside to cool.

Next, preheat your oven to 375°F and line a baking sheet with parchment paper. Roll out the empanada dough on a lightly floured surface to 1/8-inch thickness. Cut the dough into 4-inch rounds. Spoon about 2 tablespoons of the chicken and red pepper filling onto one half of each round, leaving a 1/2-inch border around the edges. Brush the edges with the beaten egg and fold the other half of the dough over the filling, pressing the edges to seal. Place the empanadas on the prepared baking sheet and brush the tops with the remaining egg.

Bake the empanadas for 20-25 minutes, or until they're golden brown and crispy.

And there you have it folks, the star of the show, the Chicken and Red Pepper Empanadas. Each flaky bite is a celebration of flavor, with juicy chicken and crisp red bell pepper taking center stage. So go ahead, grab a bite and let the good times roll!

Enjoy

<u>16</u>. Chicken and Tomato Empanadas

Prep: 30 min. Cook: 20 min. Ready in: 50 min. Servings: 4

Ingredients:

1 1/2 cups cooked and diced chicken

1 cup diced tomato

1/2 cup diced onion

1 clove of garlic, minced

1/2 teaspoon dried basil

1/2 teaspoon salt

1/4 teaspoon black pepper

1 tablespoon olive oil

1 package of empanada dough

1 egg, beaten

Cooking Directions:

Attention all food lovers! Today, we're taking a classic combination and giving it a tasty twist. Get ready for the delicious flavors of chicken and tomato in every bite of these Chicken and Tomato Empanadas.

To start, heat the olive oil in a large skillet over medium heat. Add the onion and cook until soft and translucent, about 5 minutes. Then, add the minced garlic and cook for another minute. Add the diced chicken and cook for another 2-3 minutes. Stir in the tomato, basil, salt, and pepper, and cook for another minute. Set aside to cool.

Next, preheat your oven to 375°F and line a baking sheet with parchment paper. Roll out the empanada dough on a lightly floured surface to 1/8-inch thickness. Cut the dough into 4-inch rounds. Spoon about 2 tablespoons of the chicken and tomato filling onto one half of each round, leaving a 1/2-inch border around the edges. Brush the edges with the beaten egg and fold the other half of the dough over the filling, pressing the edges to seal. Place the empanadas on the prepared baking sheet and brush the tops with the remaining egg. Bake the empanadas for 20-25 minutes, or until they're golden brown and crispy.

And there you have it, a delicious empanada filled with the flavors of chicken and tomato. Each bite is packed with juicy and tender chicken, and the freshness of tomato. So go ahead, grab a bite and enjoy the taste of these delicious empanadas!

Enjoy

17. Chicken and Mushroom Empanadas

Prep: 20 min. Cook: 20 min. Ready in: 40 min. Servings: 4

Ingredients:

Store-bought empanada dough (8 discs)

1 cup cooked chicken, shredded

1/2 cup mushrooms, chopped

1/2 small onion, finely chopped

1 clove garlic, minced

1/4 cup shredded cheese (mozzarella or cheddar)

1 tablespoon olive oil

1/4 teaspoon cumin

1/4 teaspoon paprika

1/8 teaspoon salt

1/8 teaspoon black pepper

1 egg, beaten (for egg wash)

Cooking Directions:

Ah, Chicken and Mushroom Empanadas, a delightful marriage of flavors encased in a tender, flaky dough that'll have your taste buds dancing like a tango under a moonlit Argentine sky. These savory pastries are perfect for parties, picnics, or as an exquisite midnight snack after a long day of culinary adventures.

In a large skillet, heat the olive oil over medium heat. Add the chopped onions and garlic, and sauté until the onions become translucent and the garlic is fragrant, about 3 to 5 minutes. Toss in the chopped mushrooms and cook for another 5 minutes, until they release their moisture and begin to brown. Add the shredded chicken, cumin, paprika, salt, and black pepper to the skillet. Stir well, ensuring the spices evenly coat the chicken and mushroom mixture. Cook for another 2 to 3 minutes, then remove from heat and set aside to cool. Preheat your oven to 400°F (200°C) and line a baking sheet with parchment paper. Roll out the store-bought empanada dough and cut out circles about 5 inches in diameter. You can use a round cookie cutter or an appropriately sized bowl as a guide. Place a spoonful of the cooled chicken and mushroom filling in the center of each dough circle, and top it off with a sprinkle of shredded cheese. Fold the dough over the filling, creating a half-moon shape, and press the edges together with your fingers to seal. You can use a fork to create a decorative pattern around the edges if you'd like. Arrange the filled empanadas on the prepared baking sheet. Brush the tops with the beaten egg to give them a gorgeous golden sheen. Bake the empanadas for 20 to 25 minutes, or until they're golden brown and crispy. Allow them to cool for a few minutes before diving into your delectable creation.

Enjoy

18. Chicken and Zucchini Empanadas

Prep: 15 min. Cook: 30 min. Ready In: 45 min. Servings: 4

Ingredients:

All-purpose flour for dusting

1/2-pound cooked chicken, diced

1/2 cup diced zucchini

1/4 cup diced onion

1/4 cup diced red bell pepper

1/4 cup diced green bell pepper

2 cloves garlic, minced

1/4 cup chopped fresh cilantro leaves

1 tablespoon olive oil

Salt and ground black pepper to taste

1 cup shredded Monterey Jack cheese

4 large eggs, beaten

1 (15 ounce) package empanada dough or store-bought pie crust

---

Cooking Directions:

Empanadas, empanadas, empanadas. I can't get enough of these tasty little pockets of goodness. And these chicken and zucchini empanadas, they're something special. The combination of tender chicken and fresh zucchini is just fantastic. So, fire up the oven and let's get to work.

Preheat oven to 375 degrees F (190 degrees C).

In a large skillet, heat olive oil over medium heat. Add onion, red bell pepper, green bell pepper, and garlic. Cook and stir until vegetables are tender. Stir in cilantro. Season with salt and pepper.

Remove skillet from heat. Stir in chicken and shredded cheese. Add beaten eggs and mix well.

Roll out empanada dough on a lightly floured surface to about 1/8-inch thickness. Cut into 4-inch circles.

Place a heaping tablespoon of filling on one half of each circle. Fold dough over filling, and press edges to seal. Crimp edges with a fork to ensure a tight seal.

Place empanadas on a baking sheet.

Bake in the preheated oven for 20 to 25 minutes, or until golden brown.

And there you have it folks, chicken and zucchini empanadas. These are best served hot, but they're also great at room temperature. So go ahead, grab one, or two, or three. And as always, enjoy your meal.

Enjoy

19. Chicken and Cauliflower Empanadas

Prep: 15 min. Cook: 20 min. Ready In: 35 min. Servings: 4

Ingredients:

All-purpose flour for dusting

1 package store-bought empanada dough

2 cups cooked chicken, diced

1 cup cooked and mashed cauliflower

1/4 cup diced onion

1/4 cup diced bell pepper

1/4 cup diced jalapeño pepper

1/4 cup shredded cheddar cheese

Salt and pepper

1 egg, beaten

Cooking Directions:

Empanadas, a true global dish, adaptable to any flavor and ingredients. Today, we're going to be making something special, Chicken and Cauliflower Empanadas. Perfect for a quick lunch or a snack, these babies are packed with flavor and easy to make. So, let's get started.

Preheat the oven to 375 degrees F (190 degrees C). Line a baking sheet with parchment paper.

Dust a clean surface with flour and roll out the empanada dough to 1/8-inch thickness.

In a medium bowl, combine the chicken, mashed cauliflower, onion, bell pepper, jalapeño pepper, cheddar cheese, salt, and pepper.

Place a heaping tablespoon of the filling onto one half of each round of dough, leaving a 1/2-inch border around the edges.

Brush the edges of the dough with the beaten egg, then fold the dough over the filling and press the edges to seal.

Place the empanadas on the prepared baking sheet and brush the tops with the remaining egg.

Bake for 20 minutes, or until golden brown.

And there you have it folks, Chicken and Cauliflower Empanadas. These little pockets of deliciousness are perfect for any occasion, whether it's a quick lunch or a snack. So, go ahead and give them a try, and let me know what you think. Bon Appetit!

Enjoy

20. Chicken and Broccoli Empanadas

Prep: 20 min. Cook: 20 min. Ready In: 40 min. Servings: 4

Ingredients:

1-pound boneless, skinless chicken breasts, diced

1/2 cup diced onion

1/2 cup diced red bell pepper

1/4 cup diced jalapeno pepper

1 cup chopped broccoli florets

1/4 teaspoon cayenne pepper

1/4 teaspoon black pepper

1/4 teaspoon salt

1/4 cup grated cheddar cheese

1/4 cup grated Monterey Jack cheese

1 package (15 oz) store-bought empanada dough

1 large egg, beaten with 1 tablespoon water

Cooking Directions:

Alright folks, get ready for a treat, these Chicken and Broccoli Empanadas are going to be a hit.

First things first, preheat your oven to 375 degrees F. Next, heat a skillet over medium-high heat and cook the chicken until browned, about 5 minutes. Remove the chicken from the skillet with a slotted spoon and set it aside. Add the onion, red bell pepper, jalapeno pepper and broccoli to the skillet, and cook until softened, about 5 minutes. Stir in the cayenne pepper, black pepper, and salt. Cook for another minute. Stir in the chicken, cheddar cheese and Monterey Jack cheese into the skillet, cook until cheese melted.

Now it's time to assemble the empanadas. Roll out the empanada dough on a lightly floured surface to about 1/8-inch thickness. Cut the dough into 4-inch circles using a round cookie cutter or the rim of a glass. Spoon about 2 tablespoons of the chicken and broccoli filling onto one half of each dough circle, leaving a 1/2-inch border around the edges. Brush the beaten egg around the edges of the dough, then fold the dough over the filling to form a half-moon shape. Press the edges together to seal.

Place the empanadas on a baking sheet and brush the tops with the remaining beaten egg. Bake for 20 minutes, or until golden brown.

Serve hot, garnished with fresh chopped parsley, or with a spicy salsa on the side. And don't forget a cold beer because these empanadas are going to be a hit.

Enjoy

21. Chicken and Spinach Empanadas

Prep: 20 min. Cook: 20 min. Ready in: 40 min. Servings: 4

Ingredients:

1 lb. boneless, skinless chicken breasts, diced

1 onion, diced

3 cloves of garlic, minced

1 cup of frozen spinach, thawed and drained

1/4 cup of cilantro, chopped

1/4 cup of parsley, chopped

1/4 cup of diced green olives

2 tablespoons of olive oil

1 teaspoon of ground cumin

1/2 teaspoon of ground paprika

Salt and pepper, to taste

1 package of store-bought empanada dough

1 egg, beaten (for egg wash)

Cooking Directions:

Alright folks, listen up. I'm going to show you how to make some damn good empanadas.

First thing you're going to do is heat up 2 tablespoons of olive oil in a pan over medium-high heat. Once that oil is hot, toss in your diced chicken and cook it until it's nice and browned. While that's happening, finely dice up a medium onion and mince 3 cloves of garlic. Once the chicken is cooked, toss in the onions and garlic, and cook for a couple of minutes until they're softened. Next up, add in 1 cup of thawed and drained spinach, 1/4 cup of chopped cilantro, 1/4 cup of chopped parsley, 1/4 cup of diced green olives, 1 teaspoon of ground cumin, and 1/2 teaspoon of ground paprika. Cook that mixture for another 2-3 minutes until everything is well combined. Season with salt and pepper to taste. Now, it's time to assemble the empanadas. Preheat your oven to 375 degrees F. Roll out the store-bought empanada dough and cut it into circles. Place a heaping spoonful of the chicken and spinach filling onto one half of each dough circle. Brush the edges with beaten egg and fold the other half of the dough over the filling to create a half-moon shape. Press the edges together to seal the empanada. Once all your empanadas are assembled, brush them with a little bit of the beaten egg and place them on a baking sheet. Bake them in the preheated oven for 20 minutes or until they're golden brown and crispy.
And there you have it, folks. A delicious and easy recipe for Chicken and Spinach Empanadas that will knock the socks off your dinner guests. Don't be afraid to experiment with different fillings, and always remember good food is all about taking risks. And these empanadas are a risk worth taking.

Enjoy

22. Chipotle Chicken Empanadas

Prep: 15 min. Cook: 25 min. Ready in: 40 min. Servings: 4

Ingredients:

3/4 lb. shredded chicken

3/4 cup of diced chipotle pepper

1/2 onion, diced

1 1/2 cloves of garlic, minced

1/2 tsp of cumin powder

Salt and pepper to taste

3/4 package of empanada dough (store-bought or homemade)

3/4 egg, beaten (for egg wash)

Cooking Directions:

Alright folks, listen up. We're going to take a walk on the spicy side with these Chipotle chicken Empanadas. And trust me, it's a flavor explosion in your mouth.

In a pan, brown the shredded chicken over medium-high heat. Add in some diced onion, minced garlic, and a teaspoon of cumin powder. Give it a good stir and let those aromatics release their flavors. Season that with some salt and pepper, and you're on your way to flavor town.

Add in some diced chipotle pepper. Remove from heat and let it cool down before you start assembling your empanadas.

Next, roll out your empanada dough. I like mine to be about 1/8 inch thick. Cut out some circles. Place a tablespoon of filling on one side of the dough circle. Brush the edges of the dough with the beaten egg. Fold the dough over the filling, forming a half-moon shape and press the edges to seal.

Place the empanadas on a baking sheet lined with parchment paper. Brush the top with the beaten egg. Bake those bad boys in the oven at 375F (190C) for 20-25 minutes or until golden brown. Serve 'em up nice and warm, maybe with some sour cream or guacamole on the side.

And there you have it folks, the perfect Chipotle chicken Empanadas.

Enjoy

23. Jerk Chicken Empanadas

Prep: 30 min. Cook: 30 min. Ready In: 60 min. Servings: 4

Ingredients:

Store-bought empanada dough (12 discs)

2 boneless, skinless chicken breasts, diced

2 tablespoons jerk seasoning (store-bought or homemade)

1 tablespoon olive oil

1/2 cup onion, finely chopped

1/2 cup bell pepper, finely chopped

1/2 cup tomatoes, diced

1/4 cup fresh cilantro, chopped

1/2 teaspoon salt

1/4 teaspoon black pepper

1 egg, beaten (for egg wash)

Cooking Directions:

Add a spicy kick to your mealtime with these tantalizing Jerk Chicken Empanadas. The enticing combination of tender, seasoned chicken, crisp vegetables, and fresh herbs creates a mouthwatering treat that's perfect for any occasion. Whether you serve them as a delectable appetizer or a satisfying main course, these empanadas are sure to impress.

In a medium bowl, mix the diced chicken breasts with the jerk seasoning. Ensure the chicken is well coated with the seasoning. Set aside to marinate for at least 15 minutes, or for better results, up to 2 hours in the refrigerator. In a large skillet, heat the olive oil over medium heat. Add the marinated chicken and cook, stirring occasionally, for about 7 to 10 minutes, or until the chicken is cooked through and lightly browned. Transfer the cooked chicken to a plate and set it aside. In the same skillet, add the chopped onion and bell pepper. Cook, stirring occasionally, for about 5 minutes, or until the vegetables are tender. Add the diced tomatoes, cooked chicken, chopped cilantro, salt, and black pepper to the skillet. Stir well to combine the ingredients. Cook for an additional 3 to 5 minutes, then remove the skillet from the heat and allow the mixture to cool.

Preheat your oven to 400°F (200°C) and line a baking sheet with parchment paper. Roll out the store-bought empanada dough and cut out circles about 5 inches in diameter. You can use a round cookie cutter or an appropriately sized bowl as a guide.

Place a spoonful of the jerk chicken filling in the center of each dough circle. Fold the dough over the filling, creating a half-moon shape, and press the edges together with your fingers to seal. You can use a fork to create a decorative pattern around the edges if you'd like. Arrange the filled empanadas on the prepared baking sheet. Brush the tops with the beaten egg to give them a gorgeous golden sheen.

Bake the empanadas for 20 to 25 minutes, or until they're golden brown and crispy. Allow them to cool for a few minutes before serving.

Enjoy

24. Chicken Fajita Empanadas

Prep: 30 min. Cook: 25 min. Ready In: 55 min. Servings: 4

Ingredients:

Store-bought empanada dough (12 discs)

1 tablespoon olive oil

1 pound boneless, skinless chicken breasts, thinly sliced

1/2 teaspoon salt

1/2 teaspoon black pepper

1 tablespoon taco seasoning

1 small onion, thinly sliced

1 small red bell pepper, thinly sliced

1 small green bell pepper, thinly sliced

1/2 cup shredded cheddar cheese

1/2 cup shredded Monterey Jack cheese

1 egg, beaten (for egg wash)

Cooking Directions:

Add a sizzling twist to your mealtime with these scrumptious Chicken Fajita Empanadas. The irresistible combination of tender, seasoned chicken, crisp vegetables, and gooey, melted cheese creates a mouthwatering treat that's perfect for any occasion. Whether you serve them as a delicious appetizer or a satisfying main course, these empanadas are sure to be a hit.

In a large skillet, heat the olive oil over medium heat. Add the thinly sliced chicken breasts, season with salt, black pepper, and taco seasoning. Cook, stirring occasionally, for 5 to 7 minutes, or until the chicken is cooked through and lightly browned. Transfer the cooked chicken to a plate and set aside. In the same skillet, add the thinly sliced onion and bell peppers. Cook, stirring occasionally, for about 5 minutes, or until the vegetables are tender and slightly caramelized.
Return the cooked chicken to the skillet and stir well to combine the ingredients. Remove the skillet from the heat and allow the mixture to cool. Preheat your oven to 400°F (200°C) and line a baking sheet with parchment paper. Roll out the store-bought empanada dough and cut out circles about 5 inches in diameter. You can use a round cookie cutter or an appropriately sized bowl as a guide.
Place a spoonful of the chicken fajita filling in the center of each dough circle, followed by a sprinkle of both cheddar and Monterey Jack cheese. Fold the dough over the filling, creating a half-moon shape, and press the edges together with your fingers to seal. You can use a fork to create a decorative pattern around the edges if you'd like.
Arrange the filled empanadas on the prepared baking sheet. Brush the tops with the beaten egg to give them a gorgeous golden sheen.
Bake the empanadas for 20 to 25 minutes, or until they're golden brown and crispy. Allow them to cool for a few minutes before serving.

Enjoy

25. Buffalo Chicken Empanadas

Prep: 30 min. Cook: 25 min. Ready In: 55 min. Servings: 4

Ingredients:

Store-bought empanada dough (12 discs)

1 tablespoon olive oil

1 pound boneless, skinless chicken breasts, diced

1/2 teaspoon salt

1/2 teaspoon black pepper

1/3 cup buffalo sauce, plus more for drizzling

1/4 cup crumbled blue cheese

1/2 cup shredded mozzarella cheese

2 green onions, thinly sliced

1 egg, beaten (for egg wash)

Cooking Directions:

Indulge in a flavor explosion with these lip-smacking Buffalo Chicken Empanadas. The mouthwatering combination of tender, spicy chicken, tangy blue cheese, gooey mozzarella, and zesty green onions creates an irresistible treat that's perfect for any occasion. Whether you serve them as a delectable appetizer or a satisfying main course, these empanadas are sure to impress.

In a large skillet, heat the olive oil over medium heat. Add the diced chicken breasts, season with salt and black pepper, and cook, stirring occasionally, for 7 to 10 minutes, or until the chicken is cooked through and lightly browned. Transfer the cooked chicken to a plate and set aside. In a medium bowl, mix the cooked chicken with the buffalo sauce, ensuring that the chicken is well coated.

Preheat your oven to 400°F (200°C) and line a baking sheet with parchment paper. Roll out the store-bought empanada dough and cut out circles about 5 inches in diameter. You can use a round cookie cutter or an appropriately sized bowl as a guide.

Place a spoonful of the buffalo chicken filling in the center of each dough circle, followed by a sprinkle of crumbled blue cheese, shredded mozzarella, and a few green onion slices.

Fold the dough over the filling, creating a half-moon shape, and press the edges together with your fingers to seal. You can use a fork to create a decorative pattern around the edges if you'd like.

Arrange the filled empanadas on the prepared baking sheet. Brush the tops with the beaten egg to give them a gorgeous golden sheen.

Bake the empanadas for 20 to 25 minutes, or until they're golden brown and crispy. Allow them to cool for a few minutes before serving.

If desired, drizzle additional buffalo sauce over the empanadas before serving for an extra kick of flavor.

Enjoy

26. BBQ Pork Empanadas

Prep: 15 min. Cook: 20 min. Ready in: 35 min. Servings: 4

Ingredients:

3/4 lb. of pulled pork

1/2 cup of BBQ sauce

1/2 onion, diced

1 clove of garlic, minced

1/4 tsp of smoked paprika

Salt and pepper to taste

3/4 package of empanada dough (store-bought or homemade)

3/4 egg, beaten (for egg wash)

Cooking Directions:

Alright folks, if you're looking for a party in your mouth, you've come to the right place. These BBQ Pork Empanadas are the perfect blend of savory and smoky flavors that will have you coming back for more. Let's get started, shall we?

In a pan, sauté some diced onion and minced garlic until softened. Add in some pulled pork, 1/4 cup of BBQ sauce, and a 1/4 tsp of smoked paprika. Give it a good stir, season it with some salt and pepper. Remove from heat and let it cool down before you start assembling your empanadas.

Next, roll out your empanada dough. I like mine to be about 1/8 inch thick. Cut out some circles. Place a tablespoon of filling on one side of the dough circle. Brush the edges of the dough with the beaten egg. Fold the dough over the filling, forming a half-moon shape and press the edges to seal.

Place the empanadas on a baking sheet lined with parchment paper. Brush the top with the beaten egg. Bake those bad boys in the oven at 375F (190C) for 15-20 minutes or until golden brown. Serve 'em up nice and warm, maybe with some coleslaw on the side.

And there you have it folks, the perfect BBQ Pork Empanadas.

Enjoy

27. Pork and Apricot Empanadas

Prep: 45 min. Cook: 30 min. Ready In: 1 h. 15 min. Servings: 4

Ingredients:

1 lb. pork shoulder, cut into small cubes

1 onion, diced

3 cloves of garlic, minced

1 cup of diced apricots

1 teaspoon of smoked paprika

1 teaspoon of cumin

1 teaspoon of salt

1/2 teaspoon of black pepper

1/4 cup of slivered almonds

1/4 cup of green olives, sliced

1/4 cup of cilantro, chopped

1 package of store-bought empanada dough

1 egg, beaten

Cooking Directions:

Empanadas, my dear friends, are the ultimate comfort food. They're warm, flaky and can be filled with just about anything. Today, we're going to show you how to make pork and apricot empanadas that will change the way you think about empanadas. Trust me, these are not your grandma's empanadas.

In a large skillet, brown the pork over medium-high heat until it's cooked through. Drain any excess fat.

Add the onion and garlic to the skillet and cook until softened, about 5 minutes. Stir in the diced apricots, smoked paprika, cumin, salt, and black pepper. Cook for an additional 5 minutes. Stir in the slivered almonds, green olives, and cilantro. Cook for a final 2 minutes. Remove from heat and let cool. Preheat the oven to 375 degrees F (190 degrees C). Roll out the store-bought empanada dough on a lightly floured surface. Cut into circles using a cookie cutter or a glass.

Place a spoonful of the pork and apricot mixture on one half of each empanada dough circle. Brush the edges of the dough with the beaten egg. Fold the dough over the filling to create a half-moon shape and press the edges together to seal. Place the empanadas on a baking sheet and brush the tops with the remaining beaten egg.

Bake for 20-25 minutes, or until golden brown.

And there you have it, folks. Pork and apricot empanadas that will make your taste buds sing. Serve them up with some chimichurri or aioli and enjoy. Trust me, these are the real deal. Buen provecho!

Enjoy

28. Pork and Cabbage Empanadas

Prep: 30 min. Cook: 20 min. Ready in: 50 min. Servings: 4

Ingredients:

1 pound ground pork

1/2 cup diced onion

1/2 cup shredded cabbage

1/2 teaspoon dried thyme

1/2 teaspoon salt

1/4 teaspoon black pepper

1 tablespoon olive oil

1 package of empanada dough

1 egg, beaten

Cooking Directions:

Ladies and gentlemen, gather around, because I've got a treat for you. These Pork and Cabbage Empanadas are the stuff of legends. The juicy ground pork and crisp cabbage, encased in a flaky, golden crust, are sure to tantalize your taste buds and leave you coming back for more. So let's dive in, shall we?

To start, heat the olive oil in a large skillet over medium heat. Add the onion and cook until soft and translucent, about 5 minutes. Then, add the ground pork and cook until browned, about 7-8 minutes. Stir in the cabbage, thyme, salt, and pepper, and cook for another 2-3 minutes. Set aside to cool.

Next, preheat your oven to 375°F and line a baking sheet with parchment paper. Roll out the empanada dough on a lightly floured surface to 1/8-inch thickness. Cut the dough into 4-inch rounds. Spoon about 2 tablespoons of the pork and cabbage filling onto one half of each round, leaving a 1/2-inch border around the edges. Brush the edges with the beaten egg and fold the other half of the dough over the filling, pressing the edges to seal. Place the empanadas on the prepared baking sheet and brush the tops with the remaining egg.

And there you have it, folks! These Pork and Cabbage Empanadas are the perfect way to enjoy a comforting, flavorful meal. So go ahead, grab one (or two, we won't judge), sit back, and savor each bite. These empanadas are the epitome of handheld heaven.

Enjoy

29. Curried Pork Empanada

Prep: 30 min. Cook: 20 min. Ready in: 50 min. Servings: 4

Ingredients:

1 pound ground pork

1/2 cup diced onion

2 tablespoons yellow curry powder

1/2 teaspoon salt

1/4 teaspoon black pepper

1 tablespoon olive oil

1 package of empanada dough

1 egg, beaten

Cooking Directions:

Ladies and gentlemen, gather around for a taste of the exotic! These Curried Pork Empanadas are a flavor extravaganza, with juicy ground pork and bold curry spices encased in a flaky, golden crust.

To start, heat the olive oil in a large skillet over medium heat. Add the onion and cook until soft and translucent, about 5 minutes. Then, add the ground pork and cook until browned, about 8-10 minutes. Stir in the curry powder, salt, and pepper, and cook for another 2-3 minutes. Set aside to cool.

Next, preheat your oven to 375°F and line a baking sheet with parchment paper. Roll out the empanada dough on a lightly floured surface to 1/8-inch thickness. Cut the dough into 4-inch rounds. Spoon about 2 tablespoons of the curried pork filling onto one half of each round, leaving a 1/2-inch border around the edges. Brush the edges with the beaten egg and fold the other half of the dough over the filling, pressing the edges to seal. Place the empanadas on the prepared baking sheet and brush the tops with the remaining egg.

Bake the empanadas for 20-25 minutes, or until they're golden brown and crispy.

And there you have it folks, the flavor adventure, the Curried Pork Empanadas. Each flaky bite is a journey to the East, with juicy ground pork and bold curry spices taking center stage. So go ahead, grab a bite, and let the good times roll!

Enjoy

30. Pork and Apple Empanadas

Prep: 15 min. Cook: 20 min. Ready in: 35 min. Servings: 4

Ingredients:

1 lb. ground pork

1 granny smith apple, peeled and diced

1/2 onion, diced

1/4 cup raisins

1/4 cup chopped cilantro

1 tsp cumin

1/2 tsp smoked paprika

1/4 tsp salt

1/4 tsp pepper

1 package of empanada wrappers (8-12 wrappers)

1 egg, beaten for egg wash

oil for frying

Cooking Directions:

Alright, let's get our hands dirty and make some bloody delicious Pork and Apple Empanadas. This recipe will serve 4 people, so let's make sure we have enough ingredients.

First, we're going to start by browning the ground pork in a pan over medium heat. Once it's cooked through, add in the diced onion and apple. Cook for a few minutes until the onion is translucent. Next, add in the raisins, cilantro, cumin, smoked paprika, salt, and pepper. Give it a good stir and let it cook for another 5 minutes. Remove from heat and let it cool.

While the pork mixture cools, take your empanada wrappers, and place a spoonful of the mixture on one half of the wrapper. Brush the edges with the beaten egg and fold the wrapper in half to create a half-moon shape. Press the edges to seal the empanada. Repeat this process until you have used up all the pork mixture.

Now, in a deep pan or a fryer, heat up some oil to 350 degrees F. Carefully add the empanadas and fry them for about 2-3 minutes on each side, or until golden brown.

Remove from the oil and let them cool for a few minutes. These Pork and Apple Empanadas are bloody perfect as a snack or an appetizer, but you can also serve them with a nice green salad for a complete meal. Enjoy, you bloody legends!

Enjoy

31. Pork and Pineapple Empanadas

Prep: 30 min. Cook: 2 h Ready in: 2 h 30 min. Servings: 4

Ingredients:

1 pound pork shoulder, diced
1/2 cup diced pineapple
1/4 cup diced red onion
1/4 cup diced red bell pepper
1/4 cup diced green bell
pepper
1/4 cup diced yellow bell
pepper
1/4 cup diced jalapeño pepper
1/4 cup diced cilantro
1/4 cup diced green onion
1/4 cup diced garlic
1/4 cup diced ginger
1/4 cup diced tomato
1/4 cup diced chicken stock
1/4 cup diced nutmeg
1/4 cup diced allspice
1/4 cup diced cloves
1/4 cup diced bay leaves
1/4 cup diced thyme
1/4 cup diced oregano
1/4 cup diced marjoram
1/4 cup diced rosemary
1/4 cup diced basil
1/4 cup diced parsley
1/4 cup diced cilantro
1/4 cup diced green onion
1 package of store-bought
empanada dough

1/4 cup diced pineapple juice
1/4 cup diced soy sauce
1/4 cup diced sake
1/4 cup diced olive oil
1/4 cup diced cornstarch
1/4 cup diced water
1/4 cup diced sugar
1/4 cup diced salt
1/4 cup diced black pepper
1/4 cup diced cumin
1/4 cup diced paprika
1/4 cup diced chili powder
1/4 cup diced cayenne pepper
1/4 cup diced cinnamon

Cooking Directions:

Listen up, kids, this one's a little bit of a project, but trust me when I say it's worth it. These Pork and Pineapple Empanadas are going to knock your socks off.

First thing's first, let's get our pork diced up nice and small. We're going to give it a little bath in a marinade made of pineapple juice, soy sauce, sake, olive oil, and all those spices I listed off earlier. Let that sit in the fridge for at least an hour, but overnight is even better. While the pork's marinating, we're going to start prepping our filling. Take a look at that list of vegetables I gave you, we're going to dice all that up nice and small. Once that's done, we're going to sauté it all in a pan with a little bit of oil, and then mix it in with our pork. We're going to let that simmer on low heat for about an hour and a half, or until the pork is nice and tender.

Once the filling is done, we're going to roll out our store-bought empanada dough, and start filling and folding those bad boys. Make sure to crimp the edges nice and tight so none of that filling falls out. Pop those empanadas in the oven at 350 degrees for about 15-20 minutes, or until the dough is nice and golden brown. And just like that, you've got yourself some damn fine Pork and Pineapple Empanadas. Serve it up with a cold beer and enjoy!

Enjoy

32. Pork and Blue Berry Empanadas

Prep: 15 min. Cook: 30 min. Ready In: 45 min. Servings: 4

Ingredients:

All-purpose flour for dusting

1/2-pound cooked pork, diced

1/4 cup diced onion

1/4 cup diced red bell pepper

1/4 cup diced green bell pepper

1/2 cup fresh blueberries

2 cloves garlic, minced

1/4 cup chopped fresh cilantro leaves

1 tablespoon olive oil

Salt and ground black pepper to taste

1 cup shredded Monterey Jack cheese

4 large eggs, beaten

1 (15 ounce) package empanada dough or store-bought pie crust

Cooking Directions:

Empanadas, empanadas, empanadas. I love empanadas. The flaky crust, the savory filling. And these pork and blueberry empanadas, well they're something special. The sweetness of the blueberries and the savory pork, it's a unique and delicious combination. So, fire up the oven and let's get to work.

Preheat oven to 375 degrees F (190 degrees C).

In a large skillet, heat olive oil over medium heat. Add onion, red bell pepper, green bell pepper, and garlic. Cook and stir until vegetables are tender. Stir in cilantro. Season with salt and pepper.

Remove skillet from heat. Stir in pork, blueberries, and shredded cheese. Add beaten eggs and mix well.

Roll out empanada dough on a lightly floured surface to about 1/8-inch thickness. Cut into 4-inch circles.

Place a heaping tablespoon of filling on one half of each circle. Fold dough over filling, and press edges to seal. Crimp edges with a fork to ensure a tight seal.

Place empanadas on a baking sheet.

Bake in the preheated oven for 20 to 25 minutes, or until golden brown.

And there you have it folks, pork and blueberry empanadas. Although it's not a traditional combination of ingredients, it's a unique and delicious flavor. These are best served hot, but they're also great at room temperature. So go ahead, grab one, or two, or three. And as always, enjoy your meal.

Enjoy

33. Pork and Pineapple Empanadas

Prep: 20 min. Cook: 20 min. Ready in: 40 min. Servings: 4

Ingredients:

Store-bought empanada dough (12 discs)

1 1/2 cups cooked beef, shredded (preferably from a slow-cooked roast or brisket)

1/2 cup BBQ sauce (choose your favorite)

1 small onion, finely chopped

1/4 cup bell pepper, finely chopped

2 cloves garlic, minced

2 tablespoons olive oil

1/4 teaspoon salt

1/4 teaspoon black pepper

1 egg, beaten (for egg wash)

Cooking Directions:

Feast your senses on the smoky, succulent flavors of these BBQ Beef Empanadas. This Tex-Mex inspired twist on traditional empanadas combines tender, slow-cooked beef with rich, tangy BBQ sauce, all tucked inside a flaky, golden pastry. Perfect for sharing with friends at a backyard cookout or satisfying your cravings during a cozy movie night, these empanadas will surely become a favorite.

In a large skillet, heat the olive oil over medium heat. Add the chopped onions, bell pepper, and garlic, and sauté until the onions become translucent and the garlic is fragrant, about 3 to 5 minutes. Add the shredded beef to the skillet and stir well. Pour in the BBQ sauce and continue to cook, stirring occasionally, until the beef is heated through and the flavors meld together, about 5 to 7 minutes. Season with salt and pepper, then remove from heat and let the mixture cool. Preheat your oven to 400°F (200°C) and line a baking sheet with parchment paper. Roll out the store-bought empanada dough and cut out circles about 5 inches in diameter. You can use a round cookie cutter or an appropriately sized bowl as a guide. Place a spoonful of the cooled BBQ beef filling in the center of each dough circle. Fold the dough over the filling, creating a half-moon shape, and press the edges together with your fingers to seal. You can use a fork to create a decorative pattern around the edges if you'd like. Arrange the filled empanadas on the prepared baking sheet. Brush the tops with the beaten egg to give them a gorgeous golden sheen. Bake the empanadas for 20 to 25 minutes, or until they're golden brown and crispy. Allow them to cool for a few minutes before serving.

<u>Enjoy</u>

34. Pork and Apple Empanadas

Prep: 30 min. Cook: 20 min. Ready in: 50 min. Servings: 4

Ingredients:

1 pound ground pork

1 large Granny Smith apple, peeled, cored, and diced

1/2 cup diced onion

1/2 teaspoon dried thyme

1/2 teaspoon salt

1/4 teaspoon black pepper

1 tablespoon olive oil

1 package of empanada dough

1 egg, beaten

Cooking Directions:

Ah, the humble empanada, a staple in kitchens all over the world. Each bite of these Pork and Apple Empanadas is a flavor explosion, with juicy ground pork and sweet, tart apples nestled inside a flaky, golden crust. So, let's get cooking, shall we?

To start, heat the olive oil in a large skillet over medium heat. Add the onion and cook until soft and translucent, about 5 minutes. Then, add the ground pork and cook until browned, about 7-8 minutes. Stir in the apples, thyme, salt, and pepper, and cook for another 2-3 minutes. Set aside to cool.

Next, preheat your oven to 375°F and line a baking sheet with parchment paper. Roll out the empanada dough on a lightly floured surface to 1/8-inch thickness. Cut the dough into 4-inch rounds. Spoon about 2 tablespoons of the pork and apple filling onto one half of each round, leaving a 1/2-inch border around the edges. Brush the edges with the beaten egg and fold the other half of the dough over the filling, pressing the edges to seal. Place the empanadas on the prepared baking sheet and brush the tops with the remaining egg.

Bake the empanadas for 20-25 minutes, or until they're golden brown and crispy. Serve warm and…

Enjoy

35. Breakfast Sausage and Potato Empanadas

Prep: 20 min. Cook: 30 min. Ready In: 50 min. Servings: 4

Ingredients:

Store-bought empanada dough (12 discs)

1/2 lb breakfast sausage, casings removed

1 tablespoon olive oil

1 cup potatoes, diced small

1/2 cup onion, finely chopped

1/2 cup bell pepper, finely chopped

1/2 teaspoon salt

1/4 teaspoon black pepper

1 cup shredded cheddar cheese

1 egg, beaten (for egg wash)

Cooking Directions:

Start your day off right with these scrumptious Breakfast Sausage and Potato Empanadas. The enticing combination of savory sausage, tender potatoes, and gooey cheddar cheese creates a mouthwatering treat that's perfect for any morning. Whether you serve them as a delicious breakfast or a satisfying brunch, these empanadas are sure to impress.

In a large skillet, cook the breakfast sausage over medium heat, breaking it up into small pieces with a spatula. Cook until it's browned and cooked through, about 5 to 7 minutes. Transfer the cooked sausage to a plate and set it aside. In the same skillet, heat the olive oil over medium heat. Add the diced potatoes, chopped onion, and chopped bell pepper. Season with salt and black pepper. Cook, stirring occasionally, for about 10 to 12 minutes, or until the potatoes are tender and lightly browned. Add the cooked sausage back to the skillet with the potato mixture, and stir to combine. Remove the skillet from the heat and allow the mixture to cool slightly. Once cooled, stir in the shredded cheddar cheese. Preheat your oven to 400°F (200°C) and line a baking sheet with parchment paper.

Roll out the store-bought empanada dough and cut out circles about 5 inches in diameter. You can use a round cookie cutter or an appropriately sized bowl as a guide. Place a spoonful of the sausage and potato filling in the center of each dough circle.

Fold the dough over the filling, creating a half-moon shape, and press the edges together with your fingers to seal. You can use a fork to create a decorative pattern around the edges if you'd like.

Arrange the filled empanadas on the prepared baking sheet. Brush the tops with the beaten egg to give them a gorgeous golden sheen.

Bake the empanadas for 20 to 25 minutes, or until they're golden brown and crispy. Allow them to cool for a few minutes before serving.

Enjoy

36. Chorizo and Potato Empanadas

Prep: 20 min. Cook: 20 min. Ready in: 40 min. Servings: 4

Ingredients:

Store-bought empanada dough (12 discs)

1 lb (450 g) chorizo, removed from casing and crumbled

2 cups potatoes, diced small

1 small onion, finely chopped

2 cloves garlic, minced

2 tablespoons olive oil

1/2 teaspoon smoked paprika

1/4 teaspoon salt

1/4 teaspoon black pepper

1 egg, beaten (for egg wash)

Cooking Directions:

Unleash your inner culinary adventurer with these mouthwatering Chorizo and Potato Empanadas. This scrumptious fusion of spicy chorizo and tender potatoes, all enveloped in a golden, flaky pastry, is the perfect way to kick your taste buds into high gear. Enjoy them as a hearty appetizer, a satisfying snack, or even a flavorful addition to your next brunch spread.

In a large skillet, heat the olive oil over medium heat. Add the chopped onions and garlic, and sauté until the onions become translucent and the garlic is fragrant, about 3 to 5 minutes.

Add the crumbled chorizo to the skillet and cook until it's browned and cooked through, about 5 to 7 minutes. Drain off any excess fat.

Stir in the diced potatoes and smoked paprika, and continue to cook until the potatoes are tender, about 10 minutes. Season with salt and pepper, then remove from heat and let the mixture cool.

Preheat your oven to 400°F (200°C) and line a baking sheet with parchment paper.

Roll out the store-bought empanada dough and cut out circles about 5 inches in diameter. You can use a round cookie cutter or an appropriately sized bowl as a guide.

Place a spoonful of the cooled chorizo and potato filling in the center of each dough circle.

Fold the dough over the filling, creating a half-moon shape, and press the edges together with your fingers to seal. You can use a fork to create a decorative pattern around the edges if you'd like.

Arrange the filled empanadas on the prepared baking sheet. Brush the tops with the beaten egg to give them a gorgeous golden sheen.

Bake the empanadas for 20 to 25 minutes, or until they're golden brown and crispy. Allow them to cool for a few minutes before serving.

Enjoy

37. Ham and Cheese Empanadas

Prep: 20 min. Cook: 20 min. Ready in: 40 min. Servings: 4

Ingredients:

Store-bought empanada dough (12 discs)

1 1/2 cups cooked ham, diced

1 1/2 cups shredded cheese (Swiss, Gruyère, or cheddar)

1 small onion, finely chopped

2 tablespoons Dijon mustard

2 tablespoons mayonnaise

1 tablespoon olive oil

1/4 teaspoon black pepper

1 egg, beaten (for egg wash)

Cooking Directions:

Take a trip down memory lane with these delightful Ham and Cheese Empanadas, a classic combination that never goes out of style. These savory parcels of gooey cheese and succulent ham, all wrapped up in a golden, flaky pastry, are the perfect comfort food for any occasion. Enjoy them as an appetizer, a casual snack, or a satisfying lunchtime treat.

In a large mixing bowl, combine the diced ham, shredded cheese, Dijon mustard, and mayonnaise. Mix well, ensuring that the ingredients are evenly distributed. Set aside. In a small skillet, heat the olive oil over medium heat. Add the chopped onion and cook until it becomes translucent and slightly golden, about 3 to 5 minutes. Remove from heat and let the onions cool. Add the cooled onions and black pepper to the ham and cheese mixture, and stir well to incorporate. Preheat your oven to 400°F (200°C) and line a baking sheet with parchment paper. Roll out the store-bought empanada dough and cut out circles about 5 inches in diameter. You can use a round cookie cutter or an appropriately sized bowl as a guide.

Place a spoonful of the ham and cheese filling in the center of each dough circle. Fold the dough over the filling, creating a half-moon shape, and press the edges together with your fingers to seal. You can use a fork to create a decorative pattern around the edges if you'd like. Arrange the filled empanadas on the prepared baking sheet. Brush the tops with the beaten egg to give them a gorgeous golden sheen.

Bake the empanadas for 20 to 25 minutes, or until they're golden brown and crispy. Allow them to cool for a few minutes before serving.

Enjoy

38. Turkey and Gravy Empanadas

Prep: 15 min. Cook: 30 min. Ready In: 45 min. Servings: 4

Ingredients:

All-purpose flour for dusting

1 package store-bought empanada dough

2 cups cooked turkey, diced

1/4 cup diced onion

1/4 cup diced celery

1/4 cup diced carrots

1/4 cup turkey gravy

Salt and pepper

1 egg, beaten

Cooking Directions:

Empanadas, the ultimate way to use up leftovers. And today, we're going to be making something that's going to make your Thanksgiving leftovers sing, Turkey and Gravy Empanadas. These bad boys are packed with flavor and perfect for a quick lunch or a snack. So, let's get started.

Preheat the oven to 375 degrees F (190 degrees C). Line a baking sheet with parchment paper.

Dust a clean surface with flour and roll out the empanada dough to 1/8-inch thickness.

In a medium bowl, combine the turkey, onion, celery, carrots, gravy, salt, and pepper.

Place a heaping tablespoon of the filling onto one half of each round of dough, leaving a 1/2-inch border around the edges.

Brush the edges of the dough with the beaten egg, then fold the dough over the filling and press the edges to seal.

Place the empanadas on the prepared baking sheet and brush the tops with the remaining egg.

Bake for 20 minutes, or until golden brown.

And there you have it folks, Turkey and Gravy Empanadas. These little pockets of deliciousness are the perfect way to use up those Thanksgiving leftovers. So, go ahead and give them a try, and let me know what you think. Bon Appetit!

Enjoy

39. Turkey and Cranberry Empanadas

Prep: 30 min. Cook: 20 min. Ready in: 50 min. Servings: 4

Ingredients:

1 package of store-bought empanada dough

1 cup of cooked turkey, diced

1/4 cup of cranberry sauce

1/4 cup of chopped scallions

1/4 cup of shredded cheese

Salt and pepper, to taste

1 egg, beaten (for egg wash)

Cooking Directions:

Listen up folks, I got a recipe for you that's going to change the game. These Turkey and Cranberry Empanadas are a perfect way to use up that leftover turkey from Thanksgiving. I'm talking tender, juicy turkey combined with tangy cranberry sauce, and a hint of scallions and cheese, all wrapped up in a flaky, golden-brown crust.

First things first, preheat that oven to 375 degrees. Trust me, you don't want to skimp on the heat. Next, take that cooked turkey and dice it up, throw it in a mixing bowl with cranberry sauce, scallions, cheese, and season with salt and pepper to taste.

Now, take that store-bought dough and roll it out on a floured surface. Cut out circles with a round cutter. Place a spoonful of the turkey mixture in the center of each dough circle. Fold the dough over to form a half-moon shape and press the edges to seal. Brush the top of each empanada with beaten egg.

Place the empanadas on a baking sheet and pop them in the oven for 20 minutes, or until golden brown. Serve them up with a cold beer and enjoy the goodness.

And trust me, these empanadas will be a hit at any party or gathering. So, don't be afraid to experiment and try out different fillings, the possibilities are endless. Embrace the empanadas.

Enjoy

40. Turkey and Stuffing Empanadas

Prep: 15 min. Cook: 25 min. Ready in: 40 min. Servings: 4

Ingredients:

1/2 cup diced onion

1/2 cup diced celery

2 cloves garlic, minced

1 1/2 cups chopped cooked turkey

1 cup prepared stuffing

1/2 cup cranberry sauce

Salt and pepper, to taste

1 egg, lightly beaten

2 tablespoons water

2 (9-inch) rounds store-bought pie dough

Cooking Directions:

Now, let's get cooking! Empanadas are a classic dish from South America and are basically turnovers filled with all sorts of tasty ingredients. Today, we're making a twist on the traditional recipe by filling our empanadas with a combination of juicy turkey, savory stuffing, and tangy cranberry sauce.

To start, let's make the filling. In a skillet over medium heat, sauté the onion, celery, and garlic until softened, about 5 minutes. Add the turkey and stuffing and continue to cook for an additional 2-3 minutes, stirring occasionally. Stir in the cranberry sauce, season with salt and pepper to taste, and set aside to cool.

Next, let's assemble the empanadas. Preheat your oven to 375°F (190°C). Roll out the pie dough on a lightly floured surface to about 1/8 inch thick. Cut the dough into 4 equal pieces.

Place about 1/4 of the filling in the center of each piece of dough. Brush the edges of the dough with the beaten egg and water mixture. Fold the dough over the filling to form a half-moon shape, pressing the edges together to seal. Cut a few slits in the top of each empanada to allow steam to escape.

Bake the empanadas on a baking sheet for 25 minutes or until golden brown. Serve hot and...

Enjoy

41. Turkey and Green Beans Empanadas

Prep: 30 min. Cook: 20 min. Ready in: 50 min. Servings: 4

Ingredients:

1 1/2 cups cooked and diced turkey

1 cup cooked green beans, diced

1/2 cup diced onion

1 clove of garlic, minced

1/2 teaspoon dried thyme

1/2 teaspoon salt

1/4 teaspoon black pepper

1 tablespoon olive oil

1 package of empanada dough

1 egg, beaten

Cooking Directions:

Step right up, folks! Today, we're serving up a taste sensation with these Turkey and Green Beans Empanadas. Get ready for a flavor-packed journey with every bite.

To start, heat the olive oil in a large skillet over medium heat. Add the onion and cook until soft and translucent, about 5 minutes. Then, add the minced garlic and cook for another minute. Add the diced turkey and cook for another 2-3 minutes. Stir in the green beans, thyme, salt, and pepper, and cook for another minute. Set aside to cool.

Next, preheat your oven to 375°F and line a baking sheet with parchment paper. Roll out the empanada dough on a lightly floured surface to 1/8-inch thickness. Cut the dough into 4-inch rounds. Spoon about 2 tablespoons of the turkey and green bean filling onto one half of each round, leaving a 1/2-inch border around the edges. Brush the edges with the beaten egg and fold the other half of the dough over the filling, pressing the edges to seal. Place the empanadas on the prepared baking sheet and brush the tops with the remaining egg. Bake the empanadas for 20-25 minutes, or until they're golden brown and crispy.

And there you have it, a delicious empanada filled with the flavors of turkey and green beans. Each bite is packed with juicy and tender turkey, and the crunch of green beans. So go ahead, grab a bite and enjoy the taste of these delicious empanadas!

<u>Enjoy</u>

42. Turkey and Cranberry Empanadas

Prep: 30 min. Cook: 20 min. Ready in: 50 min. Servings: 4

Ingredients:

1 1/2 cups cooked, diced turkey

1/2 cup cranberry sauce

1/2 cup diced onion

1/2 teaspoon dried thyme

1/2 teaspoon salt

1/4 teaspoon black pepper

1 tablespoon olive oil

1 package of empanada dough

1 egg, beaten

Cooking Directions:

Ladies and gentlemen, gather around for a taste of the holidays! These Turkey and Cranberry Empanadas are a festive twist on the classic empanada, with juicy turkey and sweet cranberries encased in a flaky, golden crust.

To start, heat the olive oil in a large skillet over medium heat. Add the onion and cook until soft and translucent, about 5 minutes. Then, add the diced turkey and cook for another 2-3 minutes. Stir in the cranberry sauce, thyme, salt, and pepper, and cook for another minute. Set aside to cool. Next, preheat your oven to 375°F and line a baking sheet with parchment paper. Roll out the empanada dough on a lightly floured surface to 1/8-inch thickness. Cut the dough into 4-inch rounds. Spoon about 2 tablespoons of the turkey and cranberry filling onto one half of each round, leaving a 1/2-inch border around the edges. Brush the edges with the beaten egg and fold the other half of the dough over the filling, pressing the edges to seal. Place the empanadas on the prepared baking sheet and brush the tops with the remaining egg. Bake the empanadas for 20-25 minutes, or until they're golden brown and crispy.

And that's a wrap folks! These Turkey and Cranberry Empanadas are the perfect addition to any holiday feast. With juicy, savory turkey and sweet, tangy cranberries all tucked inside a flaky, golden crust, each bite is a celebration of flavor and holiday cheer. So go ahead, make a batch of these empanadas, and let the festivities begin!

Enjoy

43. Tuna and Olive Empanada

Prep: 30 min. Cook: 30 min. Ready in: 60 min. Servings: 4

Ingredients:

1 cup all-purpose flour

1/2 teaspoon salt

1/4 cup cold butter, diced

1/4 cup cold shortening, diced

1/4 cup ice water

1 can (7 ounces) tuna, drained

1/4 cup chopped green olives

1/4 cup chopped pimiento-stuffed olives

1/4 cup chopped onion

1 egg yolk, lightly beaten

Cooking Directions:

Alright folks, listen up. This recipe for Tuna and Olive Empanadas is a classic, it's simple and it's delicious. It's going to take you about 30 minutes to prep, and another 30 minutes to cook. But trust me, it's worth the wait.

First things first, let's make the dough. In a large mixing bowl, combine the flour and salt. Cut in the butter and shortening until the mixture resembles coarse crumbs. Gradually add the ice water, stirring with a fork until the dough forms a ball. Cover and refrigerate for 30 minutes.

Now, while that's chillin', let's get the filling together. In a medium mixing bowl, combine the tuna, olives, onion, and pimiento. Mix well.

When the dough is chilled, roll it out into a large circle on a lightly floured surface. Using a round cutter or a glass, cut the dough into 4-inch circles.

Now, this is the fun part. Take one of the circles and spoon a heaping tablespoon of the tuna mixture onto one half of the circle. Brush the edge with the egg yolk, then fold the dough over and press the edges together to seal. Repeat with the remaining dough and filling.

Place the empanadas on a baking sheet and brush them with the remaining egg yolk. Pop them in a preheated 350 degrees F oven for about 30 minutes, or until golden brown.

Serve them hot and enjoy, folks. These empanadas are the perfect combination of salty and savory. They're a classic dish that everyone should try at least once in their life.

Enjoy

44. Tuna and Green Olive Empanadas

Prep: 20 min. Cook: 20 min. Ready in: 40 min. Servings: 4

Ingredients:

1 can of tuna in oil, drained

1/4 cup of chopped green olives

1/4 cup of diced onion

2 cloves of garlic, minced

1/4 cup of chopped fresh cilantro

Salt and pepper, to taste

1 package of store-bought empanada dough

1 egg, beaten, for egg wash

Cooking Directions:

Alright folks, gather round, I got a recipe that's going to knock your socks off. Tuna and Green Olive Empanadas, the perfect blend of savory and tangy. And the best part is they're easy to make, so you can impress your guests without breaking a sweat. Let's get started.

First things first, preheat that oven to 375F (190C). While that's heating up, let's get the filling ready. In a medium bowl, mix the tuna, green olives, onion, garlic, cilantro, salt, and pepper. Now, this is going to be the heart and soul of our empanadas. A good filling is the key to a good empanada. Roll out the empanada dough on a lightly floured surface. Alright, now we got our dough, it's store-bought so it's going to be easy. Roll it out nice and thin, we don't want it too thick. Use a round cookie cutter or a glass to cut out 4-inch circles. Now you got your circles, make sure they're nice and round, unless you're into that rustic look. Place a heaping tablespoon of the tuna mixture on one half of each dough circle. Now, this is where the magic happens, spoon a nice amount of the filling on one half of the circle, not too much, not too little. Leave a little bit of space around the edges. Brush the edges of the dough with the beaten egg and fold the dough over, pressing the edges together to seal. Fold it over, press the edges together, you want to make sure it's sealed good, otherwise, the filling's going to fall out. Brush the tops of the empanadas with the remaining beaten egg and make a few small slits on the top of each empanada. Brush the top with the egg wash, it's going to give it that nice golden color. And don't forget the slits, it's going to let the steam out. Place the empanadas on a baking sheet lined with parchment paper and bake for 20-25 minutes, or until golden brown. In the oven they go, 20-25 minutes and you got yourself a masterpiece. Remove from the oven and let them cool for a few minutes before serving. Take them out of the oven, let them cool for a bit, you don't want to burn your mouth, trust me.
And there you have it folks, Tuna and Green Olive Empanadas that are as delicious as they are easy to make. I guarantee they'll be a hit at your next dinner party or game night. So go ahead, impress your friends and family with your culinary skills.

45. Tuna and Red Onion Empanadas

Prep: 15 min. Cook: 20 min. Ready In: 35 min. Servings: 4

Ingredients:

1 package store-bought empanada dough

1 can of tuna, drained

1/2 red onion, finely diced

1/4 cup chopped fresh cilantro

1/4 cup raisins

1/4 cup sliced green olives

1/4 teaspoon cumin

Salt and pepper

1 egg, beaten

Cooking Directions:

Empanadas, those delicious little pockets of heaven filled with all sorts of goodies. Today, we're going to be making something special, Tuna and Red Onion Empanadas. Perfect for a quick lunch or a snack, these babies are packed with flavor and easy to make. So, let's get started.

Preheat the oven to 375 degrees F (190 degrees C). Line a baking sheet with parchment paper.

Dust a clean surface with flour and roll out the empanada dough to 1/8-inch thickness.

In a medium bowl, combine the tuna, red onion, cilantro, raisins, olives, cumin, salt, and pepper.

Place a heaping tablespoon of the filling onto one half of each round of dough, leaving a 1/2-inch border around the edges.

Brush the edges of the dough with the beaten egg, then fold the dough over the filling and press the edges to seal.

Place the empanadas on the prepared baking sheet and brush the tops with the remaining egg.

Bake for 20 minutes, or until golden brown.

And there you have it folks, Tuna, and Red Onion Empanadas. These little pockets of deliciousness are perfect for any occasion, whether it's a quick lunch or a snack. So, go ahead and give them a try, and let me know what you think. Bon Appetit!

Enjoy

46. Tuna and Red Pepper Empanadas

Prep: 20 min. Cook: 20 min. Ready in: 40 min. Servings: 4

Ingredients:

4 pie crusts

2 cans of tuna, drained

1 red bell pepper, diced

1/4 cup diced onion

1 clove garlic, minced

1 tsp dried oregano

Salt and pepper to taste

1 egg, beaten

2 tbsp olive oil

Cooking Directions:

Alright folks, grab your aprons and let's get cookin'! Today, we're making Tuna and Red Pepper Empanadas, a flavorful and hearty dish that's perfect for lunch or dinner. With store-bought pie crust dough and a few simple ingredients, we're going to create a dish that's easy to make and absolutely delicious.

Alright, let's start by preheating our oven to 400°F.

In a pan, we're going to heat up some olive oil over medium heat, and then add in some minced garlic, diced onion, and diced red bell pepper. Cook until those veggies are nice and soft, about 5 minutes.

Next, we'll add in our drained tuna, along with some dried oregano, and some salt and pepper to taste. Cook for another 2-3 minutes, until everything is well combined. And then, remove from heat and let it cool.

We're gonna take our store-bought pie crust and cut it into 4 equal pieces. Roll each piece into a circle, about 7-8 inches in diameter.

Spoon some of the tuna mixture onto one half of each pie crust circle, leaving about a half inch of space around the edges. Brush the edges with a beaten egg, and then fold the other half of the pie crust over the filling, pressing the edges together to seal.

Place the empanadas on a baking sheet lined with parchment paper, and brush the top of each empanada with the remaining beaten egg.

Pop 'em in the oven and bake for 15-20 minutes, or until the crust is nice and golden brown.

And there you have it, folks! Tuna and Red Pepper Empanadas that are easy to make and packed with flavor. Serve hot with your favorite dipping sauce on the side.

Enjoy

47. Tuna and Sesame Empanadas

Prep: 30 min. Cook: 20 min. Ready in: 50 min. Servings: 4

Ingredients:

1 can of tuna, drained and flaked

1/2 cup diced onion

1 tablespoon toasted sesame seeds

1/2 teaspoon dried basil

1/2 teaspoon salt

1/4 teaspoon black pepper

1 tablespoon olive oil

1 package of empanada dough

1 egg, beaten

Cooking Directions:

Ladies and gentlemen, gather around for a taste of the ocean! These Tuna and Sesame Empanadas are a flavor sensation, with juicy tuna and nutty sesame seeds encased in a flaky, golden crust.

To start, heat the olive oil in a large skillet over medium heat. Add the onion and cook until soft and translucent, about 5 minutes. Then, add the flaked tuna and cook for another 2-3 minutes. Stir in the sesame seeds, basil, salt, and pepper, and cook for another minute. Set aside to cool.

Next, preheat your oven to 375°F and line a baking sheet with parchment paper. Roll out the empanada dough on a lightly floured surface to 1/8-inch thickness. Cut the dough into 4-inch rounds. Spoon about 2 tablespoons of the tuna and sesame filling onto one half of each round, leaving a 1/2-inch border around the edges. Brush the edges with the beaten egg and fold the other half of the dough over the filling, pressing the edges to seal. Place the empanadas on the prepared baking sheet and brush the tops with the remaining egg. Bake the empanadas for 20-25 minutes, or until they're golden brown and crispy.

And there you have it folks, the taste of the sea, the Tuna and Sesame Empanadas. Each flaky bite is a trip to the coast, with juicy tuna and nutty sesame seeds taking center stage. So go ahead, grab a bite and let the good times roll!

Enjoy

48. Tuna and Wasabi Empanadas

Prep: 30 min. Cook: 20 min. Ready in: 50 min. Servings: 4

Ingredients:

1 1/2 cups cooked, drained, and flaked tuna

2 tablespoons wasabi paste

1/2 cup diced onion

1 clove of garlic, minced

1/2 teaspoon dried thyme

1/2 teaspoon salt

1/4 teaspoon black pepper

1 tablespoon olive oil

1 package of empanada dough

1 egg, beaten

Cooking Directions:

Are you ready for a taste sensation? Today, we're fusing the classic flavors of tuna with the heat of wasabi, all wrapped up in a flaky and golden crust. These Tuna and Wasabi Empanadas are sure to deliver a bold and tangy experience with every bite.

To start, heat the olive oil in a large skillet over medium heat. Add the onion and cook until soft and translucent, about 5 minutes. Then, add the minced garlic and cook for another minute. Add the flaked tuna and cook for another 2-3 minutes. Stir in the wasabi paste, thyme, salt, and pepper, and cook for another minute. Set aside to cool.

Next, preheat your oven to 375°F and line a baking sheet with parchment paper. Roll out the empanada dough on a lightly floured surface to 1/8-inch thickness. Cut the dough into 4-inch rounds. Spoon about 2 tablespoons of the tuna and wasabi filling onto one half of each round, leaving a 1/2-inch border around the edges. Brush the edges with the beaten egg and fold the other half of the dough over the filling, pressing the edges to seal. Place the empanadas on the prepared baking sheet and brush the tops with the remaining egg.

Bake the empanadas for 20-25 minutes, or until they're golden brown and crispy.

And there you have it, a bold and tangy empanada that's sure to satisfy your spicy cravings. Each bite is packed with juicy tuna and the heat of wasabi, making for a truly unforgettable experience. So go ahead, grab a bite and enjoy the flavors of this spicy delight!

Enjoy

49. Tuna and Artichoke Empanadas

Prep: 20 min. Cook: 20 min. Ready In: 40 min. Servings: 4

Ingredients:

Store-bought empanada dough (12 discs)

1 can (6 oz) tuna in water, drained and flaked

1 can (14 oz) artichoke hearts, drained and chopped

1/2 cup mayonnaise

1/4 cup grated Parmesan cheese

1/4 cup green onions, thinly sliced

1 tablespoon fresh lemon juice

1/4 teaspoon salt

1/4 teaspoon black pepper

1 egg, beaten (for egg wash)

Cooking Directions:

Experience a delightful medley of flavors with these Tuna and Artichoke Empanadas. Combining the richness of tuna, the earthiness of artichokes, and the tanginess of lemon, these empanadas are a sophisticated and scrumptious treat. Perfect for a light lunch or a chic appetizer, these empanadas are sure to impress.

In a large mixing bowl, combine the flaked tuna, chopped artichoke hearts, mayonnaise, grated Parmesan cheese, green onions, lemon juice, salt, and black pepper. Mix until the ingredients are evenly distributed. Preheat your oven to 400°F (200°C) and line a baking sheet with parchment paper.

Roll out the store-bought empanada dough and cut out circles about 5 inches in diameter. You can use a round cookie cutter or an appropriately sized bowl as a guide.

Place a spoonful of the tuna and artichoke filling in the center of each dough circle.

Fold the dough over the filling, creating a half-moon shape, and press the edges together with your fingers to seal. You can use a fork to create a decorative pattern around the edges if you'd like.

Arrange the filled empanadas on the prepared baking sheet. Brush the tops with the beaten egg to give them a gorgeous golden sheen.

Bake the empanadas for 20 to 25 minutes, or until they're golden brown and crispy. Allow them to cool for a few minutes before serving.

And there you have it – Tuna and Artichoke Empanadas that are a true taste sensation. Share these delectable delights with friends and family or savor them on your own as a luxurious treat. With their exquisite flavor combination and elegant presentation, these empanadas are proof that sometimes, the best things in life come in small packages.

Enjoy

50. Tuna and Cucumber Empanadas

Prep: 20 min. Cook: 20 min. Ready In: 40 min. Servings: 4

Ingredients:

All-purpose flour, for dusting

1-pound store-bought empanada dough

1 can (6 ounces) tuna, drained and flaked

1/4 cup diced cucumber

1/4 cup diced red onion

1/4 cup diced red bell pepper

1/4 cup diced green bell pepper

1/4 cup diced jalapeño pepper

2 cloves garlic, minced

1/4 cup chopped fresh cilantro

1/4 cup mayonnaise

1/4 cup sour cream

1/2 teaspoon ground cumin

1/2 teaspoon smoked paprika

1/4 teaspoon salt

1/4 teaspoon black pepper

1 egg, beaten

Cooking Directions:

Empanadas are the ultimate street food, and this tuna and cucumber version is no exception. These flaky, golden-brown pockets of deliciousness are packed with flavor, and are perfect for a quick and easy lunch or dinner. And the best part? You can use store-bought dough, so you don't have to worry about making it from scratch. Let's get started.

Preheat your oven to 375°F (190°C). Line a baking sheet with parchment paper. On a lightly floured surface, roll out the empanada dough to 1/8-inch thickness.

In a medium bowl, combine the tuna, cucumber, red onion, red and green bell peppers, jalapeño, garlic, cilantro, mayonnaise, sour cream, cumin, smoked paprika, salt, and black pepper. Mix well.

Spoon about 2 tablespoons of the tuna mixture onto one half of each dough round, leaving a 1/2-inch border around the edges. Brush the edges with the beaten egg. Fold the dough over the filling, pressing the edges to seal. Crimp the edges with a fork to seal.

Place the empanadas on the prepared baking sheet. Brush the top of each empanada with the beaten egg.

Bake for 20 minutes, or until golden brown.

And there you have it, folks. Tuna and cucumber empanadas that are sure to satisfy. Serve them hot out of the oven and enjoy with a cold beer. Trust me, you won't regret it.

Enjoy

51. Shrimp and Mango Empanadas

Prep: 40 min. Cook: 20 min. Ready in: 60 min. Servings: 12

Ingredients:

3/4 lb. of cooked shrimp, peeled and diced

3/4 cup of diced mango

1/2 onion, diced

1 clove of garlic, minced

1/4 tsp of cumin

Salt and pepper to taste

3/4 package of empanada dough (store-bought or homemade)

3/4 egg, beaten (for egg wash)

Cooking Directions:

Alright folks, listen up. We're going to take a walk on the sweet and savory side with these Shrimp and Mango Empanadas. And trust me, it's a flavor explosion in your mouth.

In a pan, sauté some diced onion and minced garlic until softened. Add in some diced cooked shrimp, diced mango, 1/4 tsp of cumin, season it with some salt and pepper. Remove from heat and let it cool down before you start assembling your empanadas.

Next, roll out your empanada dough. I like mine to be about 1/8 inch thick. Cut out some circles. Place a tablespoon of filling on one side of the dough circle. Brush the edges of the dough with the beaten egg. Fold the dough over the filling, forming a half-moon shape and press the edges to seal.

Place the empanadas on a baking sheet lined with parchment paper. Brush the top with the beaten egg. Bake those bad boys in the oven at 375F (190C) for 15-20 minutes or until golden brown. Serve 'em up nice and warm, maybe with some sour cream on the side.

And there you have it folks, the perfect Shrimp and Mango Empanadas. So go ahead, indulge in the sweet and savory flavors, and enjoy the taste of these delicious treats. Embrace the sweet and savory combination and get ready to fall in love. Embrace the tropical flavors and enjoy the perfect balance of sweet and savory.

Enjoy

52. Shrimp and Scallop Empanadas

Prep: 15 min. Cook: 20 min. Ready in: 35 min. Servings: 4

Ingredients:

8 oz cooked shrimp, chopped

8 oz cooked scallops, chopped

1/2 onion, diced

1/4 cup chopped cilantro

1/4 cup diced red pepper

1/4 tsp salt

1/4 tsp cumin

1/4 tsp smoked paprika

1 package of empanada wrappers

1 egg, beaten for egg wash

oil for frying

Cooking Directions:

Alright, folks, gather around, we're going to make some empanadas that will make you want to pack your bags and travel the world.

First, we're going to take the shrimp and scallops, the jewels of the sea and chop them up. In a pan over medium heat, sauté the shrimp and scallops with diced onion, cilantro, red pepper, salt, cumin, and a pinch of smoked paprika until everything is well combined and heated through. Remove from heat and let it cool.

Now, take your empanada wrappers and place a spoonful of the seafood mixture on one half of the wrapper. Brush the edges with the beaten egg and fold the wrapper in half to create a half-moon shape. Press the edges to seal the empanada. Repeat this process until you have used up all the seafood mixture.

Now, we're going to deep fry these bad boys, so in a deep pan or a fryer, heat up some oil to 350 degrees F. Carefully add the empanadas and fry them for about 2-3 minutes on each side, or until golden brown. Trust me, the smell of the frying empanadas will make your mouth water and transport you to a beachside shack in the Caribbean.

Enjoy

53. Shrimp and Mushroom Empanadas

Prep: 20 min. Cook: 30 min. Ready in: 50 min. Servings: 4

Ingredients:

1 lb. shrimp, peeled and deveined

1/2 lb. mushrooms, sliced

1/2 small onion, diced

3 cloves garlic, minced

1/4 cup chopped cilantro

1/2 teaspoon smoked paprika

1/4 teaspoon cayenne pepper

1/2 teaspoon salt

1/4 teaspoon black pepper

1 egg, beaten

1 package of store-bought empanada dough

Cooking Directions:

Listen up folks, this recipe for Shrimp and Mushroom Empanadas is about to elevate your game. I'm talking crispy, flaky dough with a filling that's packed with flavor. It's a party in your mouth, and you're the host.

First things first, let's get the filling going. Heat a large skillet over medium-high heat and add a little bit of oil. Once that's hot, toss in your shrimp. Cook them for about 2 minutes on each side, or until they're pink and cooked through. Remove them from the skillet and set them aside.

Next up, the mushrooms. Throw 'em in the skillet and cook them until they're nice and brown. Add the onions and garlic, and cook for another 2 minutes, or until they're soft. Stir in the cilantro, smoked paprika, cayenne pepper, salt, and black pepper.

Now, it's time to bring it all together. Chop up the cooked shrimp and add it to the mushroom mixture. Mix everything together until it's well combined.

Time to roll out your dough. Dust your work surface with a little bit of flour and roll out the dough to about 1/8-inch thickness. Cut out circles of dough, about 4 inches in diameter.

Brush the edges of the dough circles with the beaten egg. Place a heaping tablespoon of the shrimp and mushroom mixture in the center of each circle. Fold the dough over and press the edges together to seal. Brush the top of each empanada with more beaten egg.

Pop 'em in the oven at 375 degrees F for 20 minutes, or until they're golden brown and crispy. And that, my friends, is how you make empanadas that'll make your taste buds sing.

Serve them up with a cold beer!

Enjoy

54. Shrimp and Tomato Empanadas

Prep: 20 min. Cook: 20 min. Ready In: 40 min. Servings: 4

Ingredients:

1 pound of raw shrimp, peeled and deveined

1/2 cup diced onion

2 cloves of minced garlic

1/2 cup diced tomatoes

1/4 cup chopped cilantro

1/2 teaspoon smoked paprika

1/4 teaspoon cumin

Salt and pepper to taste

1 egg, beaten

Store-bought empanada dough

Cooking Directions:

Listen up folks, you want a taste of something truly special? These shrimp and tomato empanadas are where it's at. Trust me, I've traveled the world and I know my empanadas. So, fire up the stove and let's get cooking.

In a skillet, heat the olive oil over medium heat. Add the onion and garlic and cook until softened, about 5 minutes.

Add the shrimp and cook until they turn pink, about 3 minutes.

Stir in the diced tomatoes, cumin, smoked paprika, and salt. Cook for an additional 5 minutes, or until the mixture has thickened.

Remove from heat and stir in the chopped cilantro.

Preheat the oven to 375°F.

Roll out the empanada dough on a lightly floured surface.

Cut the dough into 4-inch circles.

Place about 2 tablespoons of the shrimp mixture on one half of each circle. Brush the edges with the beaten egg.

Fold the dough over the filling to form a half-moon shape and press the edges with a fork to seal.

Brush the top with the beaten egg.

Place the empanadas on a baking sheet and bake for about 20 minutes, or until golden brown.

Alright, the timer just went off and these bad boys are looking beautiful. Crispy on the outside, hot, and juicy on the inside. Perfection. Serve them up with a cold beer and enjoy. Bon appétit!

Enjoy

55. Shrimp and Bell Pepper Empanadas

Prep: 30 min. Cook: 20 min. Ready In: 50 min. Servings: 4

Ingredients:

1 lb. of raw shrimp, peeled and deveined

1/2 onion, diced

1/2 cup of diced red bell pepper

1/2 cup of diced green bell pepper

1/4 cup of cilantro, chopped

1 teaspoon of cumin

1/2 teaspoon of chili powder

1/2 teaspoon of salt

1/4 teaspoon of black pepper

1/4 cup of grated queso fresco

1 package of store-bought empanada dough

1 egg, beaten

Cooking Directions:

Empanadas, my dear friends, are the ultimate party food. They're easy to make, easy to eat, and can be filled with just about anything. Today, we're going to show you how to make some Shrimp and Bell Pepper Empanadas that will impress your guests and leave them wanting more. Trust me, these empanadas are something special.

In a medium skillet, sauté the onion and bell peppers over medium heat until softened, about 5 minutes. Stir in the shrimp, cilantro, cumin, chili powder, salt, and black pepper. Cook until the shrimp are pink and cooked through, about 5 minutes. Stir in the queso fresco. Cook for a final 2 minutes. Remove from heat and let cool. Preheat the oven to 375 degrees F (190 degrees C). Roll out the store-bought empanada dough on a lightly floured surface. Cut into circles using a cookie cutter or a glass. Place a spoonful of the shrimp and bell pepper mixture on one half of each empanada dough circle. Brush the edges of the dough with the beaten egg. Fold the dough over the filling to create a half-moon shape and press the edges together to seal.

Place the empanadas on a baking sheet and brush the tops with the remaining beaten egg.

Bake for 15-20 minutes, or until golden brown.

And there you have it, folks. Shrimp and Bell Pepper Empanadas that will make your taste buds sing. Serve them up with some salsa or guacamole and enjoy. Trust me, these are the real deal. Buen provecho!

Enjoy

56. Shrimp and Garlic Empanadas

Prep: 15 min. Cook: 30 min. Ready In: 45 min. Servings: 4

Ingredients:

All-purpose flour for dusting

1/2-pound cooked shrimp, peeled and deveined

1/4 cup diced onion

1/4 cup diced red bell pepper

1/4 cup diced green bell pepper

2 cloves garlic, minced

1/4 cup chopped fresh cilantro leaves

1 tablespoon olive oil

Salt and ground black pepper to taste

1 cup shredded Monterey Jack cheese

4 large eggs, beaten

1 (15 ounce) package empanada dough or store-bought pie crust

---

Cooking Directions:

Empanadas, empanadas, empanadas. I've had my fair share of these delicious pockets of goodness, and let me tell you, these shrimp and garlic empanadas are something special. The combination of succulent shrimp and fragrant garlic is a match made in heaven. So, let's get to work and make some empanadas.

Preheat oven to 375 degrees F (190 degrees C).

In a large skillet, heat olive oil over medium heat. Add onion, red bell pepper, green bell pepper and garlic. Cook and stir until vegetables are tender. Stir in cilantro. Season with salt and pepper.

Remove skillet from heat. Stir in shrimp and shredded cheese. Add beaten eggs and mix well.

Roll out empanada dough on a lightly floured surface to about 1/8-inch thickness. Cut into 4-inch circles.

Place a heaping tablespoon of filling on one half of each circle. Fold dough over filling, and press edges to seal. Crimp edges with a fork to ensure a tight seal.

Place empanadas on a baking sheet.

Bake in the preheated oven for 20 to 25 minutes, or until golden brown.

And there you have it folks, shrimp and garlic empanadas that are sure to be a hit at any gathering. These are best served hot, but they're also great at room temperature. So go ahead, grab one, or two, or three. And as always, enjoy your meal.

Enjoy

57. Salmon and Garlic Empanadas

Prep: 30 min. Cook: 20 min. Ready in: 50 min. Servings: 4

Ingredients:

1 pound salmon, cooked and flaked

1/2 cup diced onion

2 cloves garlic, minced

1/2 teaspoon dried dill

1/2 teaspoon salt

1/4 teaspoon black pepper

1 tablespoon olive oil

1 package of empanada dough

1 egg, beaten

Cooking Directions:

Ladies and gentlemen, hold onto your taste buds! These Salmon and Garlic Empanadas are about to take you on a flavor journey like no other. The juicy salmon and pungent garlic are nestled inside a flaky, golden crust, making each bite a true delight.

To start, heat the olive oil in a large skillet over medium heat. Add the onion and cook until soft and translucent, about 5 minutes. Then, add the garlic and cook for another minute. Stir in the salmon, dill, salt, and pepper, and cook for another 2-3 minutes. Set aside to cool.

Next, preheat your oven to 375°F and line a baking sheet with parchment paper. Roll out the empanada dough on a lightly floured surface to 1/8-inch thickness. Cut the dough into 4-inch rounds. Spoon about 2 tablespoons of the salmon and garlic filling onto one half of each round, leaving a 1/2-inch border around the edges. Brush the edges with the beaten egg and fold the other half of the dough over the filling, pressing the edges to seal. Place the empanadas on the prepared baking sheet and brush the tops with the remaining egg. Bake the empanadas for 20-25 minutes, or until they're golden brown and crispy.

And there you have it folks, the salmon sensation, the Garlic and Salmon Empanadas. Each flaky bite is a celebration of the sea, with juicy salmon and pungent garlic taking center stage. So go ahead, grab a bite and let the waves of flavor wash over you!

Enjoy

58. Salmon and Soy Sauce Empanadas

Prep: 30 min. Cook: 20 min. Ready in: 50 min. Servings: 4

Ingredients:

1 1/2 cups cooked, flaked salmon

2 tablespoons soy sauce

1/2 cup diced onion

1/2 teaspoon dried thyme

1/2 teaspoon salt

1/4 teaspoon black pepper

1 tablespoon olive oil

1 clove of garlic, minced

1 tablespoon chopped fresh parsley

1 tablespoon chopped fresh cilantro

1 package of empanada dough

1 egg, beaten

Cooking Directions:

Gather 'round, all you seafood lovers and empanada enthusiasts! Today, we're whipping up a delicious dish of succulent salmon, savory soy sauce, and a medley of fresh herbs and spices, all nestled inside a flaky, golden crust.

To start, heat the olive oil in a large skillet over medium heat. Add the onion and cook until soft and translucent, about 5 minutes. Then, add the minced garlic and cook for another minute. Add the flaked salmon and cook for another 2-3 minutes. Stir in the soy sauce, thyme, salt, pepper, parsley, and cilantro, and cook for another minute. Set aside to cool.

Next, preheat your oven to 375°F and line a baking sheet with parchment paper. Roll out the empanada dough on a lightly floured surface to 1/8-inch thickness. Cut the dough into 4-inch rounds. Spoon about 2 tablespoons of the salmon and soy sauce filling onto one half of each round, leaving a 1/2-inch border around the edges. Brush the edges with the beaten egg and fold the other half of the dough over the filling, pressing the edges to seal. Place the empanadas on the prepared baking sheet and brush the tops with the remaining egg.

Bake the empanadas for 20-25 minutes, or until they're golden brown and crispy.

And there you have it, a delicious and savory empanada with a burst of fresh flavor. Each flaky bite is packed with succulent salmon, savory soy sauce, and a medley of herbs and spices, making for a truly memorable experience. So go ahead, grab a bite and enjoy the flavors of this seafood delight!

Enjoy

59. Salmon and Cilantro Empanadas

Prep: 30 min. Cook: 20 min. Ready in: 50 min. Servings: 4

Ingredients:

1 1/2 cups cooked, peeled, and deveined shrimp

1/2 cup diced onion

2 tablespoons chopped fresh cilantro

1 clove of garlic, minced

1/2 teaspoon dried thyme

1/2 teaspoon salt

1/4 teaspoon black pepper

1 tablespoon olive oil

1 package of empanada dough

1 egg, beaten

Cooking Directions:

Attention all seafood fans! Today, we're taking a trip to flavor town with these Shrimp and Cilantro Empanadas. Get ready for a juicy and fresh experience, wrapped in a flaky and golden crust.

To start, heat the olive oil in a large skillet over medium heat. Add the onion and cook until soft and translucent, about 5 minutes. Then, add the minced garlic and cook for another minute. Add the cooked shrimp and cook for another 2-3 minutes. Stir in the cilantro, thyme, salt, and pepper, and cook for another minute. Set aside to cool.

Next, preheat your oven to 375°F and line a baking sheet with parchment paper. Roll out the empanada dough on a lightly floured surface to 1/8-inch thickness. Cut the dough into 4-inch rounds. Spoon about 2 tablespoons of the shrimp and cilantro filling onto one half of each round, leaving a 1/2-inch border around the edges. Brush the edges with the beaten egg and fold the other half of the dough over the filling, pressing the edges to seal. Place the empanadas on the prepared baking sheet and brush the tops with the remaining egg. Bake the empanadas for 20-25 minutes, or until they're golden brown and crispy.

And there you have it, a fresh and juicy empanada that's sure to please all your seafood cravings. Each flaky bite is packed with succulent shrimp and the bold flavor of cilantro, making for a truly unforgettable experience. So go ahead, grab a bite and enjoy the flavors of this seafood delight!

Enjoy

60. Salmon and Dill Empanadas

Prep: 15 min. Cook: 20 min. Ready in: 35 min. Servings: 4

Ingredients:

1 lb. cooked salmon, flaked

1/2 onion, diced

1/4 cup chopped dill

1/4 cup sour cream

1/4 tsp salt

1/4 tsp pepper

1 package of empanada wrappers

1 egg, beaten for egg wash

oil for frying

Cooking Directions:

Listen, I've been around the world, and I've eaten some of the most exotic and interesting dishes, but I gotta tell you, these Salmon and Dill Empanadas are something special.

First, in a mixing bowl, we're going to combine the flaked salmon, diced onion, chopped dill, sour cream, salt, and pepper. Give it a good mix, you should smell the freshness of the dill and the richness of the salmon. Now, take your empanada wrappers and place a spoonful of the salmon mixture on one half of the wrapper. Brush the edges with the beaten egg and fold the wrapper in half to create a half-moon shape. Press the edges to seal the empanada. Repeat this process until you have used up all the salmon mixture. Now, we're going to deep fry these bad boys, so in a deep pan or a fryer, heat up some oil to 350 degrees F. Carefully add the empanadas and fry them for about 2-3 minutes on each side, or until golden brown. Trust me, the smell of the frying empanadas will make your mouth water. Once they're golden brown and crispy, remove them from the oil and let them cool for a few minutes. These Salmon and Dill Empanadas are the perfect combination of flavors, the richness of the salmon, the freshness of the dill, and the creaminess of the sour cream. Serve them as a snack or an appetizer, but you can also serve them with a nice green salad for a complete meal.

But let me tell you, these empanadas are so good, you might not want to share them. But hey, that's the beauty of food, it's meant to be shared and enjoyed with the people you love. So, go ahead, make these empanadas, and enjoy them while they're hot and crispy, they're truly a delight.

Enjoy

61. Salmon and Capers Empanadas

Prep: 15 min. Cook: 30 min. Ready In: 45 min. Servings: 4

Ingredients:

1-pound cooked salmon, flaked

1/4 cup diced onion

1/4 cup diced red bell pepper

1/4 cup diced green bell pepper

1/4 cup diced yellow bell pepper

1/4 teaspoon black pepper

1/4 teaspoon salt

1/4 cup capers

1/4 cup grated cheddar cheese

1/4 cup grated Monterey Jack cheese

1 package (15 oz) store-bought empanada dough

1 large egg, beaten with 1 tablespoon water

Cooking Directions:

Get ready for a culinary journey with these Salmon and Capers Empanadas. A unique combination of flavors that will transport you to a different place with every bite. Trust me, this recipe is worth trying. Let's get cooking!

First, preheat that oven to 375 degrees F. In a skillet, sauté diced onion, red bell pepper, green bell pepper, and yellow bell pepper until softened, about 5 minutes. Next, add in the flaked salmon, black pepper, salt, and capers. Cook for another 2-3 minutes, until everything is heated through. Now, it's time to add some cheese. Stir in the cheddar cheese and Monterey Jack cheese until melted.

Now it's time to assemble the empanadas. Roll out the empanada dough on a lightly floured surface to about 1/8-inch thickness. Cut the dough into 4-inch circles using a round cookie cutter or the rim of a glass. Spoon about 2 tablespoons of the salmon and capers filling onto one half of each dough circle, leaving a 1/2-inch border around the edges. Brush the beaten egg around the edges of the dough, then fold the dough over the filling to form a half-moon shape. Press the edges together to seal. Place the empanadas on a baking sheet and brush the tops with the remaining beaten egg. Pop those bad boys in the oven and bake for 20 minutes, or until golden brown.

Serve hot, garnished with fresh chopped parsley, or with a lemony aioli on the side. And don't forget a cold beer because these empanadas are going to be a hit.

<u>Enjoy</u>

62. Salmon and Lemon Empanadas

Prep: 30 min. Cook: 20 min. Ready In: 50 min. Servings: 4

Ingredients:

1 lb. of fresh salmon fillet, skin removed and flaked

1/2 onion, diced

1/2 cup of diced red bell pepper

1/4 cup of lemon juice

1/4 cup of parsley, chopped

1 teaspoon of salt

1/4 teaspoon of black pepper

1/4 cup of grated parmesan cheese

1 package of store-bought empanada dough

1 egg, beaten

Cooking Directions:

Empanadas, my dear friends, are the ultimate party food. They're easy to make, easy to eat, and can be filled with just about anything. Today, we're going to show you how to make some Salmon and Lemon Empanadas that will make your guests ask for seconds, and maybe even thirds. Trust me, these empanadas are something special.

In a medium skillet, sauté the onion and red bell pepper over medium heat until softened, about 5 minutes. Stir in the flaked salmon, lemon juice, parsley, salt, and black pepper. Cook for an additional 2 minutes.

Stir in the parmesan cheese. Cook for a final 1 minute. Remove from heat and let cool. Preheat the oven to 375 degrees F (190 degrees C).

Roll out the store-bought empanada dough on a lightly floured surface. Cut into circles using a cookie cutter or a glass. Place a spoonful of the salmon and lemon mixture on one half of each empanada dough circle.

Brush the edges of the dough with the beaten egg. Fold the dough over the filling to create a half-moon shape and press the edges together to seal. Place the empanadas on a baking sheet and brush the tops with the remaining beaten egg.

Bake for 15-20 minutes, or until golden brown.

And there you have it, folks. Salmon and Lemon Empanadas that will make your taste buds sing. Serve them up with some lemon wedges or tartar sauce and enjoy. Trust me, these are the real deal. Buen provecho!

Enjoy

63. Smoked Salmon Empanadas

Prep: 20 min. Cook: 20 min. Ready In: 40 min. Servings: 4

Ingredients:

Store-bought empanada dough (12 discs)

8 oz smoked salmon, flaked

1/2 cup cream cheese, softened

2 tablespoons capers, drained and chopped

1/4 cup red onion, finely chopped

1/4 cup fresh dill, chopped

1 tablespoon lemon juice

1/4 teaspoon black pepper

1 egg, beaten (for egg wash)

Cooking Directions:

Dive into the exquisite flavors of the sea with these elegant Smoked Salmon Empanadas. Brimming with velvety cream cheese, zesty capers, and fragrant dill, these empanadas are the perfect appetizer or snack for a sophisticated soirée or a simple evening at home. One bite, and you'll be hooked!

In a large mixing bowl, combine the flaked smoked salmon, softened cream cheese, chopped capers, finely chopped red onion, fresh dill, lemon juice, and black pepper. Mix until the ingredients are evenly distributed, and the filling is smooth. Preheat your oven to 400°F (200°C) and line a baking sheet with parchment paper. Roll out the store-bought empanada dough and cut out circles about 5 inches in diameter. You can use a round cookie cutter or an appropriately sized bowl as a guide. Place a spoonful of the smoked salmon filling in the center of each dough circle.

Fold the dough over the filling, creating a half-moon shape, and press the edges together with your fingers to seal. You can use a fork to create a decorative pattern around the edges if you'd like.

Arrange the filled empanadas on the prepared baking sheet. Brush the tops with the beaten egg to give them a gorgeous golden sheen.

Bake the empanadas for 20 to 25 minutes, or until they're golden brown and crispy. Allow them to cool for a few minutes before serving.

And there you have it – Smoked Salmon Empanadas that are as delightful to the eye as they are to the palate. Perfect for any occasion, these delicate morsels are a wonderful way to celebrate the delectable flavors of the sea. So go ahead, indulge in a luxurious taste experience, and let these empanadas whisk you away to a world of culinary enchantment.

Enjoy

64. Crab and Avocado Empanadas

Prep: 25 min. Cook: 20 min. Ready in: 45 min. Servings: 4

Ingredients:

Store-bought empanada dough (12 discs)

1 cup cooked crab meat, shredded

1 ripe avocado, diced

1/2 cup red bell pepper, finely chopped

1/4 cup fresh cilantro, chopped

1/4 cup green onions, thinly sliced

1/4 cup mayonnaise

1 tablespoon lime juice

1/4 teaspoon salt

1/4 teaspoon black pepper

1 egg, beaten (for egg wash

Cooking Directions:

Indulge in a coastal culinary escape with these delightful Crab and Avocado Empanadas. Brimming with succulent crab, creamy avocado, and a symphony of fresh, zesty flavors, these empanadas are a seafood lover's dream come true. Whether you serve them as an appetizer, a snack, or even a light lunch, they're sure to make waves at your next meal.

In a large mixing bowl, combine the cooked crab meat, diced avocado, chopped red bell pepper, fresh cilantro, and green onions.

In a separate small bowl, whisk together the mayonnaise, lime juice, salt, and black pepper. Pour this dressing over the crab and avocado mixture, and gently fold to combine, ensuring that the ingredients are evenly coated.

Preheat your oven to 400°F (200°C) and line a baking sheet with parchment paper.

Roll out the store-bought empanada dough and cut out circles about 5 inches in diameter. You can use a round cookie cutter or an appropriately sized bowl as a guide.

Place a spoonful of the crab and avocado filling in the center of each dough circle.

Fold the dough over the filling, creating a half-moon shape, and press the edges together with your fingers to seal. You can use a fork to create a decorative pattern around the edges if you'd like.

Arrange the filled empanadas on the prepared baking sheet. Brush the tops with the beaten egg to give them a gorgeous golden sheen.

Bake the empanadas for 20 to 25 minutes, or until they're golden brown and crispy. Allow them to cool for a few minutes before serving.

Enjoy

65. Crab Rangoon Empanadas

Prep: 20 min. Cook: 20 min. Ready In: 40 min. Servings: 4

Ingredients:

Store-bought empanada dough (12 discs)

8 oz cream cheese, softened

4 oz crabmeat, drained and flaked

1/4 cup green onions, finely chopped

1 clove garlic, minced

1 teaspoon Worcestershire sauce

1/2 teaspoon soy sauce

1/4 teaspoon black pepper

1 egg, beaten (for egg wash)

Cooking oil for frying (optional)

Cooking Directions:

Indulge in the delectable fusion of flavors with these Crab Rangoon Empanadas. The delightful blend of succulent crabmeat, tangy cream cheese, and flavorful seasonings creates a mouthwatering treat that's perfect for any meal. Whether you serve them as an irresistible appetizer or a satisfying main course, these empanadas are sure to impress.

In a medium bowl, mix the softened cream cheese, flaked crabmeat, chopped green onions, minced garlic, Worcestershire sauce, soy sauce, and black pepper. Stir until the ingredients are well combined.

Roll out the store-bought empanada dough and cut out circles about 5 inches in diameter. You can use a round cookie cutter or an appropriately sized bowl as a guide.

Place a spoonful of the crab rangoon filling in the center of each dough circle.

Fold the dough over the filling, creating a half-moon shape, and press the edges together with your fingers to seal. You can use a fork to create a decorative pattern around the edges if you'd like.

If baking, preheat your oven to 400°F (200°C) and line a baking sheet with parchment paper. Arrange the filled empanadas on the prepared baking sheet. Brush the tops with the beaten egg to give them a gorgeous golden sheen. Bake the empanadas for 20 to 25 minutes, or until they're golden brown and crispy. Allow them to cool for a few minutes before serving.

If frying, heat about 1 inch of cooking oil in a deep skillet or pot over medium heat. Once the oil reaches 350°F (175°C), carefully add a few empanadas at a time and fry them for 2 to 3 minutes on each side, or until they're golden brown and crispy. Use a slotted spoon to transfer the fried empanadas to a plate lined with paper towels to drain any excess oil. Allow them to cool for a few minutes before serving.

Enjoy

66. Lobster and Cream Cheese Empanadas

Prep: 30 min. Cook: 25 min. Ready In: 55 min. Servings: 4

Ingredients:

Store-bought empanada dough (12 discs)

1 tablespoon unsalted butter

1/2 cup finely chopped onion

1 garlic clove, minced

1/2 pound cooked lobster meat, chopped into small pieces

4 ounces cream cheese, softened

1/4 teaspoon salt

1/4 teaspoon black pepper

1 tablespoon chopped fresh chives

1 egg, beaten (for egg wash)

Cooking Directions:

Indulge in the luxurious flavors of these Lobster and Cream Cheese Empanadas. The luscious combination of tender lobster, velvety cream cheese, and aromatic chives creates a delectable treat that's perfect for any special occasion. Whether you serve them as an elegant appetizer or a sumptuous main course, these empanadas are sure to impress.

In a medium skillet, melt the butter over medium heat. Add the chopped onion and cook, stirring occasionally, for 3 to 5 minutes, or until the onion is softened and slightly translucent. Add the minced garlic to the skillet and cook for an additional minute, stirring frequently. Remove the skillet from the heat and let the onion and garlic mixture cool slightly. In a medium bowl, combine the cooked lobster meat, softened cream cheese, salt, black pepper, and chopped chives. Stir in the cooled onion and garlic mixture, mixing well to combine. Preheat your oven to 400°F (200°C) and line a baking sheet with parchment paper. Roll out the store-bought empanada dough and cut out circles about 5 inches in diameter. You can use a round cookie cutter or an appropriately sized bowl as a guide.

Place a spoonful of the lobster and cream cheese filling in the center of each dough circle. Fold the dough over the filling, creating a half-moon shape, and press the edges together with your fingers to seal. You can use a fork to create a decorative pattern around the edges if you'd like.

Arrange the filled empanadas on the prepared baking sheet. Brush the tops with the beaten egg to give them a gorgeous golden sheen.

Bake the empanadas for 20 to 25 minutes, or until they're golden brown and crispy. Allow them to cool for a few minutes before serving.

Enjoy

67. Spicy Shrimp Empanadas

Prep: 25 min. Cook: 20 min. Ready In: 45 min. Servings: 4

Ingredients:

Store-bought empanada dough (12 discs)

1 lb shrimp, peeled, deveined, and chopped

1/2 cup red bell pepper, finely chopped

1/2 cup green onions, thinly sliced

1 jalapeno, seeded and minced

2 cloves garlic, minced

1/4 cup fresh cilantro, chopped

1 teaspoon smoked paprika

1 teaspoon ground cumin

1/2 teaspoon salt

1/4 teaspoon black pepper

1 tablespoon olive oil

1 egg, beaten (for egg wash)

Cooking Directions:

Turn up the heat with these mouthwatering Spicy Shrimp Empanadas. Bursting with succulent shrimp, vibrant veggies, and a kick of fiery jalapeno, these empanadas are perfect for those who like it hot! Whether you serve them as a zesty appetizer or a satisfying main course, these empanadas are sure to get your taste buds tingling.

In a large skillet, heat the olive oil over medium heat. Add the red bell pepper, green onions, and minced jalapeno, and cook for 3 to 4 minutes, or until the vegetables begin to soften.

Add the minced garlic and cook for an additional 1 minute.

Stir in the chopped shrimp, smoked paprika, ground cumin, salt, and black pepper. Cook for about 5 minutes, or until the shrimp are cooked through. Remove from heat and stir in the fresh cilantro. Let the filling cool.

Preheat your oven to 400°F (200°C) and line a baking sheet with parchment paper.

Roll out the store-bought empanada dough and cut out circles about 5 inches in diameter. You can use a round cookie cutter or an appropriately sized bowl as a guide.

Place a spoonful of the spicy shrimp filling in the center of each dough circle.

Fold the dough over the filling, creating a half-moon shape, and press the edges together with your fingers to seal. You can use a fork to create a decorative pattern around the edges if you'd like.

Arrange the filled empanadas on the prepared baking sheet. Brush the tops with the beaten egg to give them a gorgeous golden sheen.

Bake the empanadas for 20 to 25 minutes, or until they're golden brown and crispy. Allow them to cool for a few minutes before serving.

Enjoy

68. Shrimp and Ginger Empanadas

Prep: 30 min. Cook: 20 min. Ready in: 50 min. Servings: 4

Ingredients:

1 pound shrimp, cooked and peeled

1/2 cup diced onion

1 tablespoon grated fresh ginger

1/2 teaspoon dried basil

1/2 teaspoon salt

1/4 teaspoon black pepper

1 tablespoon olive oil

1 package of empanada dough

1 egg, beaten

Cooking Directions:

Ladies and gentlemen, gather around for a flavor explosion like no other! These Shrimp and Ginger Empanadas are the perfect blend of sweet and spicy, with juicy shrimp and zesty ginger encased in a flaky, golden crust.

To start, heat the olive oil in a large skillet over medium heat. Add the onion and cook until soft and translucent, about 5 minutes. Then, add the ginger and cook for another minute. Stir in the shrimp, basil, salt, and pepper, and cook for another 2-3 minutes. Set aside to cool.

Next, preheat your oven to 375°F and line a baking sheet with parchment paper. Roll out the empanada dough on a lightly floured surface to 1/8-inch thickness. Cut the dough into 4-inch rounds. Spoon about 2 tablespoons of the shrimp and ginger filling onto one half of each round, leaving a 1/2-inch border around the edges. Brush the edges with the beaten egg and fold the other half of the dough over the filling, pressing the edges to seal. Place the empanadas on the prepared baking sheet and brush the tops with the remaining egg. Bake the empanadas for 20-25 minutes, or until they're golden brown and crispy.

And there you have it folks, the flavor fiesta, the Shrimp and Ginger Empanadas. Each flaky bite is a whirlwind of flavor, with juicy shrimp and zesty ginger taking center stage. So go ahead, grab a bite and let the good times roll!

Enjoy

69. Vegetable Empanadas

Prep: 15 min. Cook: 25 min. Ready in: 40 min. Servings: 4

Ingredients:

1 cup of diced mushrooms

1 cup of diced bell pepper

1/2 cup of diced onion

1/2 cup of diced carrot

1/2 cup of diced zucchini

1/4 cup of cilantro, chopped

Salt and pepper to taste

1 package of empanada dough (store-bought or homemade)

1 egg, beaten (for egg wash)

Cooking Directions:

Alright folks, listen up. This recipe is a classic and it's going to knock your socks off. Vegetable empanadas, it's a combination of flavors that just can't be beat.

In a pan, sauté the vegetables over medium-high heat until they are tender. Add in some diced onion, minced garlic, diced mushrooms, diced bell pepper, diced carrot, and diced zucchini. Give it a good stir and let those vegetables sweat and caramelize. Season that with some salt and pepper, and you're on your way to flavor town.

Add in some cilantro for some extra color and flavor. Remove from heat and let it cool down before you start assembling your empanadas.

Next, roll out your empanada dough. I like mine to be about 1/8 inch thick. Cut out some circles. Place a tablespoon of filling on one side of the dough circle. Brush the edges of the dough with the beaten egg.

Fold the dough over the filling, forming a half-moon shape and press the edges to seal. Brush the top with the beaten egg. Place the empanadas on a baking sheet lined with parchment paper.

Pop those bad boys in the oven at 375F (190C) for 20-25 minutes or until golden brown. Serve 'em up nice and warm, maybe with some chimichurri or aji on the side.

And there you have it, folks. The perfect vegetable empanadas. Savor it, and don't be shy with the hot sauce.

Enjoy

70. Mushroom and Spinach Empanadas

Prep: 15 min. Cook: 20 min. Ready in: 35 min. Servings: 4

Ingredients:

3/4 cup of sliced mushrooms

3/4 cup of chopped spinach

1/2 onion, diced

1 clove of garlic, minced

1/4 tsp of thyme

Salt and pepper to taste

3/4 package of empanada dough (store-bought or homemade)

3/4 egg, beaten (for egg wash)

Cooking Directions:

Alright folks, if you're looking for a twist on the traditional empanada, you've come to the right place. These Mushroom and Spinach Empanadas are a delicious combination of earthy mushrooms, healthy spinach and savory spices that will elevate your empanada game. Let's get started, shall we?

In a pan, sauté some diced onion, minced garlic, and sliced mushrooms until softened. Add in some chopped spinach, a 1/4 tsp of thyme, season it with some salt and pepper. Remove from heat and let it cool down before you start assembling your empanadas.

Next, roll out your empanada dough. I like mine to be about 1/8 inch thick. Cut out some circles. Place a tablespoon of filling on one side of the dough circle. Brush the edges of the dough with the beaten egg. Fold the dough over the filling, forming a half-moon shape and press the edges to seal.

Place the empanadas on a baking sheet lined with parchment paper. Brush the top with the beaten egg. Bake those bad boys in the oven at 375F (190C) for 15-20 minutes or until golden brown. Serve 'em up nice and warm, maybe with some sour cream on the side.

And there you have it folks, the perfect Mushroom and Spinach Empanadas.

Enjoy

<u>71</u>. Cheddar and Broccoli Empanadas

Prep: 20 min. Cook: 25 min. Ready In: 45 min. Servings: 4

Ingredients:

Store-bought empanada dough (12 discs)

2 cups broccoli florets, chopped into small pieces

1/2 cup water

1 tablespoon olive oil

1 small onion, finely chopped

1 garlic clove, minced

1/2 teaspoon salt

1/4 teaspoon black pepper

1 1/2 cups shredded cheddar cheese

1 egg, beaten (for egg wash)

Cooking Directions:

Savor the irresistible combination of flavors in these Cheddar and Broccoli Empanadas. The mouthwatering blend of tender broccoli, savory onion, and sharp cheddar cheese creates a scrumptious treat that's perfect for any occasion. Whether you serve them as a delicious appetizer or a satisfying main course, these empanadas are sure to delight.

In a medium saucepan, combine the chopped broccoli and water. Bring to a boil, then reduce the heat and simmer for 3 to 4 minutes, or until the broccoli is tender. Drain the broccoli and set aside.

In a large skillet, heat the olive oil over medium heat. Add the chopped onion and cook, stirring occasionally, for 3 to 5 minutes, or until the onion is softened and slightly translucent.

Add the minced garlic, salt, and black pepper to the skillet and cook for an additional minute, stirring frequently.

Remove the skillet from the heat and stir in the cooked broccoli and shredded cheddar cheese, mixing well to combine.

Preheat your oven to 400°F (200°C) and line a baking sheet with parchment paper.

Roll out the store-bought empanada dough and cut out circles about 5 inches in diameter. You can use a round cookie cutter or an appropriately sized bowl as a guide.

Place a spoonful of the cheddar and broccoli filling in the center of each dough circle.

Fold the dough over the filling, creating a half-moon shape, and press the edges together with your fingers to seal. You can use a fork to create a decorative pattern around the edges if you'd like.

Arrange the filled empanadas on the prepared baking sheet. Brush the tops with the beaten egg to give them a gorgeous golden sheen.

Bake the empanadas for 20 to 25 minutes, or until they're golden brown and crispy. Allow them to cool for a few minutes before serving.

Enjoy

72. Sweet Potato and Black Bean Empanadas

Prep: 15 min. Cook: 20 min. Ready in: 35 min. Servings: 4

Ingredients:

3/4 cup of mashed sweet potatoes

3/4 cup of black beans

1/2 onion, diced

1 clove of garlic, minced

1/4 tsp of cumin

Salt and pepper to taste

3/4 package of empanada dough (store-bought or homemade)

3/4 egg, beaten (for egg wash)

Cooking Directions:

Alright folks, listen up. We're going to take a walk on the sweet side with these Sweet Potato and Black Bean Empanadas. And trust me, it's a flavor explosion in your mouth.

In a pan, sauté some diced onion and minced garlic until softened. Add in some mashed sweet potatoes, black beans, 1/4 tsp of cumin, season it with some salt and pepper. Remove from heat and let it cool down before you start assembling your empanadas.

Next, roll out your empanada dough. I like mine to be about 1/8 inch thick. Cut out some circles. Place a tablespoon of filling on one side of the dough circle. Brush the edges of the dough with the beaten egg. Fold the dough over the filling, forming a half-moon shape and press the edges to seal.

Place the empanadas on a baking sheet lined with parchment paper. Brush the top with the beaten egg. Bake those bad boys in the oven at 375F (190C) for 15-20 minutes or until golden brown. Serve 'em up nice and warm, maybe with some sour cream on the side.

And there you have it folks, the perfect Sweet Potato and Black Bean Empanadas. So go ahead, indulge in the sweet and savory flavors, but don't blame me if you can't stop at just one!

Enjoy

73. Black Bean and Sweet Potato Empanadas

Prep: 30 min. Cook: 15 min. Ready in: 45 min. Servings: 4

Ingredients:

1 can of black beans, drained and rinsed

1 medium sweet potato, peeled and diced

1/2 red onion, diced

1 jalapeño pepper, diced

2 cloves of garlic, minced

1 teaspoon ground cumin

1/2 teaspoon chili powder

Salt and pepper, to taste

1/4 cup cilantro, chopped

1 store-bought empanada dough

1 egg, beaten (for brushing the empanadas)

Cooking Directions:

Listen folks, these empanadas are the real deal.

We're going to start by prepping our filling. Take that sweet potato, peel it, and dice it up nice and small. That's going to give us some sweetness to balance out the heat from the jalapeño.

Next, we're going to add some diced red onion and minced garlic. These are going to give us some depth of flavor and make sure these empanadas aren't one note.

Now, we're going to add our black beans, cumin, chili powder, and a pinch of salt and pepper. Make sure everything is well combined.

Now, we're going to roll out our store-bought dough, and spoon a generous amount of our filling onto each empanada. Make sure you don't overstuff them, or they'll burst open in the oven.

Fold the dough over the filling and press the edges to seal them shut. Now, take that beaten egg and brush it over the top of each empanada.

Pop them in the oven for 20 minutes, or until they're golden brown and crispy.

And voila! You've got yourself some Black Bean and Sweet Potato Empanadas that'll knock your socks off. Serve it with some cilantro and sour cream, and you're in for a treat.

Enjoy

74. Black Bean and Corn Empanadas

Prep: 20 min. Cook: 20 min. Ready In: 40 min. Servings: 4

Ingredients:

1 can black beans, drained and rinsed

1/2 cup frozen corn

1/4 cup diced onion

1/4 cup diced red bell pepper

1/4 teaspoon cumin

1/4 teaspoon smoked paprika

1/4 teaspoon black pepper

1/4 teaspoon salt

1/4 cup grated cheddar cheese

1/4 cup grated Monterey Jack cheese

1 package (15 oz) store-bought empanada dough

1 large egg, beaten with 1 tablespoon water

Cooking Directions:

Alright folks, if you're looking for a delicious and hearty empanada recipe that's a little out of the ordinary, then look no further than these Black Bean and Corn Empanadas.

First, we're going to preheat that oven to 375 degrees F. In a skillet, sauté diced onion and red bell pepper until softened, about 5 minutes. Next, add in a can of drained and rinsed black beans, 1/2 cup of frozen corn, cumin, smoked paprika, black pepper, and salt. Cook for another 2-3 minutes, until everything is heated through. Now, it's time to add some cheese. Stir in the cheddar cheese and Monterey Jack cheese until melted. Now it's time to assemble the empanadas. Roll out the empanada dough on a lightly floured surface to about 1/8-inch thickness. Cut the dough into 4-inch circles using a round cookie cutter or the rim of a glass. Spoon about 2 tablespoons of the black bean and corn filling onto one half of each dough circle, leaving a 1/2-inch border around the edges. Brush the beaten egg around the edges of the dough, then fold the dough over the filling to form a half-moon shape. Press the edges together to seal.

Place the empanadas on a baking sheet and brush the tops with the remaining beaten egg. Pop those bad boys in the oven and bake for 20 minutes, or until golden brown.

Serve hot, garnished with fresh chopped cilantro, or with a spicy salsa on the side. And don't forget a cold beer because these empanadas are going to be a crowd pleaser.

Enjoy

75. Black Bean and Cheese Empanadas

Prep: 15 min. Cook: 20 min. Ready in: 35 min. Servings: 4

Ingredients:

1 can black beans, drained and rinsed

1/2 onion, diced

1/4 cup diced red bell pepper

1/4 cup chopped cilantro

1/4 cup diced jalapeño pepper (optional)

1 tsp cumin

1/2 tsp smoked paprika

1/4 tsp salt

1/4 tsp pepper

1 cup shredded cheddar cheese

1 package of empanada wrappers

1 egg, beaten for egg wash

oil for frying

Cooking Directions:

Get ready for some serious flavor explosion, as we're about to make some Black Bean and Cheese Empanadas that are going to knock your socks off. We'll be using a combination of black beans, onions, red bell pepper, cilantro, and spices, that will be perfectly balanced with the addition of melted cheese, all wrapped in a crispy and flaky pastry. So, preheat your fryer or a deep pan and let's begin this culinary journey.

First, we're going to start by sautéing the diced onion and red bell pepper in a pan over medium heat. Once it's cooked through, add in the black beans, cilantro, jalapeño pepper (if using), cumin, smoked paprika, salt, and pepper. Give it a good stir and let it cook for another 5 minutes. Remove from heat and let it cool.

While the black bean mixture cools, take your empanada wrappers and place a spoonful of the mixture on one half of the wrapper. Then add a good pinch of shredded cheese, Brush the edges with the beaten egg and fold the wrapper in half to create a half-moon shape. Press the edges to seal the empanada. Repeat this process until you have used up all the black bean mixture.

Now, in a deep pan or a fryer, heat up some oil to 350 degrees F. Carefully add the empanadas and fry them for about 2-3 minutes on each side, or until golden brown.

Remove from the oil and let them cool for a few minutes. These Black Bean and Cheese Empanadas are bloody perfect as a snack or an appetizer, but you can also serve them with a nice green salad for a complete meal. Enjoy, you bloody legends!

Enjoy

76. Black Bean and Avocado Empanadas

Prep: 30 min. Cook: 20 min. Ready In: 50 min. Servings: 4

Ingredients:

1 can of black beans, drained and rinsed

1/2 onion, diced

3 cloves of garlic, minced

1 avocado, diced

1 teaspoon of cumin

1/2 teaspoon of chili powder

1/2 teaspoon of salt

1/4 teaspoon of black pepper

1/4 cup of cilantro, chopped

1 package of store-bought empanada dough

1 egg, beaten

Cooking Directions:

Empanadas, my friends, are the epitome of versatile. They can be filled with just about anything and today we're going to show you how to make some Black Bean and Avocado Empanadas that will knock your socks off. These empanadas are not only delicious but also vegetarian and gluten-free, so you can enjoy them with no guilt, and no judgement.

In a medium skillet, sauté the onion and garlic over medium heat until softened, about 5 minutes. Stir in the black beans, avocado, cumin, chili powder, salt, and black pepper. Cook for an additional 5 minutes.

Stir in the cilantro. Cook for a final 2 minutes. Remove from heat and let cool. Preheat the oven to 375 degrees F (190 degrees C). Roll out the store-bought empanada dough on a lightly floured surface. Cut into circles using a cookie cutter or a glass. Place a spoonful of the black bean and avocado mixture on one half of each empanada dough circle. Brush the edges of the dough with the beaten egg. Fold the dough over the filling to create a half-moon shape and press the edges together to seal. Place the empanadas on a baking sheet and brush the tops with the remaining beaten egg. Bake for 15-20 minutes, or until golden brown.

And there you have it, folks. Black Bean and Avocado Empanadas that will make your taste buds dance. Serve them up with some salsa or guacamole and enjoy. Trust me, these are the real deal. Buen provecho!

Enjoy

77. Black Beans and Sweet Pepper Empanadas

Prep: 15 min. Cook: 30 min. Ready In: 45 min. Servings: 4

Ingredients:

All-purpose flour for dusting

1 (15 ounce) can black beans, drained and rinsed

1/4 cup diced onion

1/4 cup diced red bell pepper

1/4 cup diced green bell pepper

1/4 cup diced sweet pepper

2 cloves garlic, minced

1/4 cup chopped fresh cilantro leaves

1 tablespoon olive oil

Salt and ground black pepper to taste

1 cup shredded Monterey Jack cheese

4 large eggs, beaten

1 (15 ounce) package empanada dough or store-bought pie crust

Cooking Directions:

Empanadas, empanadas, empanadas. I've had my fair share of these delicious pockets of goodness, and I've got to say, these black bean and sweet pepper empanadas are something special. The combination of savory black beans and sweet peppers is a classic and always a crowd pleaser. So, let's get to work and make some empanadas.

Preheat oven to 375 degrees F (190 degrees C).

In a large skillet, heat olive oil over medium heat. Add onion, red bell pepper, green bell pepper, sweet pepper, and garlic. Cook and stir until vegetables are tender. Stir in cilantro. Season with salt and pepper.

Remove skillet from heat. Stir in black beans and shredded cheese. Add beaten eggs and mix well.

Roll out empanada dough on a lightly floured surface to about 1/8-inch thickness. Cut into 4-inch circles.

Place a heaping tablespoon of filling on one half of each circle. Fold dough over filling, and press edges to seal. Crimp edges with a fork to ensure a tight seal.

Place empanadas on a baking sheet.

Bake in the preheated oven for 20 to 25 minutes, or until golden brown.

And there you have it folks, black bean and sweet pepper empanadas that are sure to be a hit at any gathering. These are best served hot, but they're also great at room temperature. So go ahead, grab one, or two, or three. And as always, enjoy your meal.

Enjoy

78. Mushroom and Goat Cheese Empanadas

Prep: 35 min. Cook: 25 min. Ready in: 50 min. Servings: 4

Ingredients:

8 oz mushrooms, sliced

1/2 onion, diced

1/4 cup chopped parsley

1/4 cup crumbled goat cheese

1/4 tsp salt

1/4 tsp pepper

1 package of empanada wrappers

1 egg, beaten for egg wash

oil for frying

Cooking Directions:

Alright, folks, gather around, we're going to make some empanadas that will make your taste buds sing.

First, in a pan over medium heat, sauté the mushrooms and diced onion until the mushrooms are tender and the onion is translucent. Remove from heat and let it cool. Once it's cool, in a mixing bowl, we're going to combine the mushroom mixture, chopped parsley, crumbled goat cheese, salt, and pepper. Give it a good mix, you should smell the earthiness of the mushrooms and the tanginess of the goat cheese.

Now, take your empanada wrappers and place a spoonful of the mushroom mixture on one half of the wrapper. Brush the edges with the beaten egg and fold the wrapper in half to create a half-moon shape. Press the edges to seal the empanada. Repeat this process until you have used up all the mushroom mixture. Now, we're going to deep fry these bad boys, so in a deep pan or a fryer, heat up some oil to 350 degrees F. Carefully add the empanadas and fry them for about 2-3 minutes on each side, or until golden brown. Trust me, the smell of the frying empanadas will make your mouth water. Once they're golden brown and crispy, remove them from the oil and let them cool for a few minutes. These Mushroom and Goat Cheese Empanadas are the perfect combination of flavors, the earthiness of the mushrooms, the tanginess of the goat cheese, and the freshness of the parsley. Serve them as a snack or an appetizer, but you can also serve them with a nice green salad for a complete meal.

Enjoy

79. Cheese and Jalapeno Empanadas

Prep: 20 min. Cook: 20 min. Ready in: 40 min. Servings: 4

Ingredients:

Store-bought empanada dough (12 discs)

1 1/2 cups shredded cheese (sharp cheddar or pepper jack)

1/2 cup pickled jalapenos, chopped

1 small onion, finely chopped

2 cloves garlic, minced

2 tablespoons olive oil

1/4 teaspoon salt

1/4 teaspoon black pepper

1 egg, beaten (for egg wash)

Cooking Directions:

Add a touch of heat to your culinary repertoire with these scrumptious Cheese and Jalapeno Empanadas. The irresistible combination of gooey, melted cheese and zesty jalapenos makes for a delightful surprise in each bite, all wrapped up in a golden, flaky pastry. Perfect for a cozy gathering or an adventurous snack, these empanadas will make your taste buds dance with excitement.

In a large skillet, heat the olive oil over medium heat. Add the chopped onions and garlic, and sauté until the onions become translucent and the garlic is fragrant, about 3 to 5 minutes. Remove the skillet from heat and let the onion and garlic mixture cool for a few minutes. In a large mixing bowl, combine the shredded cheese, chopped pickled jalapenos, and the cooled onion and garlic mixture. Stir well, adding salt and pepper to taste. Preheat your oven to 400°F (200°C) and line a baking sheet with parchment paper. Roll out the store-bought empanada dough and cut out circles about 5 inches in diameter. You can use a round cookie cutter or an appropriately sized bowl as a guide. Place a spoonful of the cheese and jalapeno filling in the center of each dough circle. Fold the dough over the filling, creating a half-moon shape, and press the edges together with your fingers to seal. You can use a fork to create a decorative pattern around the edges if you'd like. Arrange the filled empanadas on the prepared baking sheet. Brush the tops with the beaten egg to give them a gorgeous golden sheen. Bake the empanadas for 20 to 25 minutes, or until they're golden brown and crispy. Allow them to cool for a few minutes before serving.

Enjoy

80. Roasted Vegetable Empanadas

Prep: 30 min. Cook: 20 min. Ready in: 50 min. Servings: 4

Ingredients:

Store-bought empanada dough (12 discs)

1 cup zucchini, diced

1 cup bell peppers (mixed colors), diced

1 cup eggplant, diced

1 cup cherry tomatoes, halved

1 small red onion, diced

2 cloves garlic, minced

1/4 cup fresh basil, chopped

1/4 cup crumbled feta cheese (optional)

3 tablespoons olive oil

1/2 teaspoon salt

1/2 teaspoon black pepper

1 egg, beaten (for egg wash)

Cooking Directions:

Celebrate the bounty of the garden with these scrumptious Roasted Vegetable Empanadas, a tasty homage to Mother Nature's finest creations. Brimming with colorful veggies, fragrant herbs, and a touch of optional tangy feta, these empanadas are a delicious way to eat your greens (and reds, yellows, and purples) in style.

Preheat your oven to 425°F (220°C). In a large bowl, combine the zucchini, bell peppers, eggplant, cherry tomatoes, red onion, and garlic. Drizzle with 2 tablespoons of olive oil, and season with salt and pepper. Toss to coat the vegetables evenly.

Spread the seasoned vegetables on a large baking sheet in a single layer. Roast in the preheated oven for 20 to 25 minutes, or until the vegetables are tender and lightly browned. Remove from the oven and let them cool.

Once the vegetables have cooled, transfer them to a large mixing bowl. Stir in the chopped basil and crumbled feta cheese (if using). Reduce the oven temperature to 400°F (200°C) and line a baking sheet with parchment paper.

Roll out the store-bought empanada dough and cut out circles about 5 inches in diameter. You can use a round cookie cutter or an appropriately sized bowl as a guide.

Place a spoonful of the roasted vegetable filling in the center of each dough circle.

Fold the dough over the filling, creating a half-moon shape, and press the edges together with your fingers to seal. You can use a fork to create a decorative pattern around the edges if you'd like.

Arrange the filled empanadas on the prepared baking sheet. Brush the tops with the beaten egg to give them a gorgeous golden sheen.

Bake the empanadas for 20 to 25 minutes, or until they're golden brown and crispy. Allow them to cool for a few minutes before serving.

Enjoy

81. Butternut Squash Empanadas

Prep: 25 min. Cook: 20 min. Ready In: 45 min. Servings: 4

Ingredients:

Store-bought empanada dough (12 discs)

2 cups butternut squash, peeled and diced

1 tablespoon olive oil

1/2 cup onion, finely chopped

2 cloves garlic, minced

1/2 teaspoon ground cumin

1/4 teaspoon ground cinnamon

1/4 teaspoon smoked paprika

1/4 teaspoon salt

1/4 teaspoon black pepper

1/2 cup crumbled feta cheese

1/4 cup fresh cilantro, chopped

1 egg, beaten (for egg wash)

Cooking Directions:

Discover the warm, comforting flavors of these Butternut Squash Empanadas. The delightful combination of tender butternut squash, aromatic spices, and tangy feta cheese creates a mouthwatering treat that's perfect for any meal. Whether you serve them as a delicious appetizer or a satisfying main course, these empanadas are sure to impress.

Preheat your oven to 400°F (200°C). Toss the diced butternut squash with olive oil and spread it out on a baking sheet. Roast for 20 to 25 minutes, or until the squash is tender and lightly caramelized. Allow the squash to cool slightly. In a large skillet, heat the olive oil over medium heat. Add the chopped onion and cook for 3 to 4 minutes, or until softened. Add the minced garlic, ground cumin, ground cinnamon, smoked paprika, salt, and black pepper to the skillet, and cook for an additional 1 to 2 minutes, or until fragrant. Stir in the roasted butternut squash, crumbled feta cheese, and chopped fresh cilantro. Mix until the ingredients are evenly distributed. Roll out the store-bought empanada dough and cut out circles about 5 inches in diameter. You can use a round cookie cutter or an appropriately sized bowl as a guide. Place a spoonful of the butternut squash filling in the center of each dough circle. Fold the dough over the filling, creating a half-moon shape, and press the edges together with your fingers to seal. You can use a fork to create a decorative pattern around the edges if you'd like. Arrange the filled empanadas on a parchment-lined baking sheet. Brush the tops with the beaten egg to give them a gorgeous golden sheen.
Bake the empanadas for 20 to 25 minutes, or until they're golden brown and crispy. Allow them to cool for a few minutes before serving.

Enjoy

82. Caramelized Onion and Goat Cheese Empanadas

Prep: 15 min. Cook: 40 min. Ready In: 55 min. Servings: 4

Ingredients:

Store-bought empanada dough (12 discs)

2 tablespoons olive oil

3 large onions, thinly sliced

1/2 teaspoon salt

1/4 teaspoon black pepper

1 tablespoon balsamic vinegar

1 tablespoon brown sugar

4 oz goat cheese, crumbled

2 tablespoons fresh thyme, chopped

1 egg, beaten (for egg wash)

Cooking Directions:

Experience the heavenly combination of sweet, savory, and tangy flavors in these Caramelized Onion and Goat Cheese Empanadas. The luscious mix of tender caramelized onions and creamy goat cheese creates a mouthwatering treat that's perfect for any occasion. Whether you serve them as a delectable appetizer or a satisfying main course, these empanadas are sure to impress.

In a large skillet, heat the olive oil over medium heat. Add the thinly sliced onions, salt, and black pepper. Cook, stirring occasionally, for about 20 minutes, or until the onions are soft and golden brown. Be sure to reduce the heat if the onions begin to burn. Add the balsamic vinegar and brown sugar to the skillet, and continue to cook for an additional 5 to 10 minutes, or until the onions are caramelized and the liquid has evaporated. Remove the skillet from the heat and allow the caramelized onions to cool. Once cooled, stir in the crumbled goat cheese and chopped fresh thyme. Preheat your oven to 400°F (200°C) and line a baking sheet with parchment paper. Roll out the store-bought empanada dough and cut out circles about 5 inches in diameter. You can use a round cookie cutter or an appropriately sized bowl as a guide. Place a spoonful of the caramelized onion and goat cheese filling in the center of each dough circle. Fold the dough over the filling, creating a half-moon shape, and press the edges together with your fingers to seal. You can use a fork to create a decorative pattern around the edges if you'd like. Arrange the filled empanadas on the prepared baking sheet. Brush the tops with the beaten egg to give them a gorgeous golden sheen.
Bake the empanadas for 20 to 25 minutes, or until they're golden brown and crispy. Allow them to cool for a few minutes before serving.

Enjoy

83. Smoked Gouda and Mushroom Empanadas

Prep: 20 min. Cook: 20 min. Ready In: 40 min. Servings: 4

Ingredients:

Store-bought empanada dough (12 discs)

1 tablespoon olive oil

1 lb mixed mushrooms, sliced (such as cremini, shiitake, and oyster)

1/2 cup onion, finely chopped

2 cloves garlic, minced

1 cup smoked Gouda cheese, grated

1/4 cup fresh parsley, chopped

1/4 teaspoon salt

1/4 teaspoon black pepper

1 egg, beaten (for egg wash)

Cooking Directions:

Indulge in the earthy, smoky goodness of these Smoked Gouda and Mushroom Empanadas. The luscious combination of tender mushrooms and rich smoked Gouda cheese creates a mouthwatering, savory treat that's perfect for any gathering. Whether you serve them as an enticing appetizer or a satisfying main course, these empanadas are sure to impress.

In a large skillet, heat the olive oil over medium heat. Add the chopped onion and cook for 3 to 4 minutes, or until softened. Add the sliced mushrooms and minced garlic to the skillet, and cook for an additional 6 to 8 minutes, or until the mushrooms are tender and have released their moisture. Remove the skillet from the heat and allow the mushroom mixture to cool. Once cooled, stir in the grated smoked Gouda cheese, chopped fresh parsley, salt, and black pepper. Preheat your oven to 400°F (200°C) and line a baking sheet with parchment paper. Roll out the store-bought empanada dough and cut out circles about 5 inches in diameter. You can use a round cookie cutter or an appropriately sized bowl as a guide. Place a spoonful of the smoked Gouda and mushroom filling in the center of each dough circle. Fold the dough over the filling, creating a half-moon shape, and press the edges together with your fingers to seal. You can use a fork to create a decorative pattern around the edges if you'd like. Arrange the filled empanadas on the prepared baking sheet. Brush the tops with the beaten egg to give them a gorgeous golden sheen. Bake the empanadas for 20 to 25 minutes, or until they're golden brown and crispy. Allow them to cool for a few minutes before serving.
And there you have it – Smoked Gouda and Mushroom Empanadas that are a deliciously decadent delight. Share these savory sensations with friends and family, or savor them solo as a luxurious treat. One bite of these empanadas, and you'll be transported to a world of rich, earthy flavors and irresistible textures.

Enjoy

84. Spinach and Feta Empanadas

Prep: 15 min. Cook: 20 min. Ready in: 35 min. Servings: 4

Ingredients:

1 cup of chopped spinach

1/2 cup of crumbled feta cheese

1/2 onion, diced

1 clove of garlic, minced

1/4 tsp of cumin powder

Salt and pepper to taste

3/4 package of empanada dough (store-bought or homemade)

3/4 egg, beaten (for egg wash)

Cooking Directions:

Alright, folks, we're going to take a walk on the Mediterranean side with these Spinach and Feta Empanadas.

In a pan, sauté some diced onion and minced garlic until softened. Add in some chopped spinach and a 1/4 tsp of cumin powder. Give it a good stir, season it with some salt and pepper. Remove from heat and let it cool down before you start assembling your empanadas.

Next, roll out your empanada dough. I like mine to be about 1/8 inch thick. Cut out some circles. Place a tablespoon of filling on one side of the dough circle. Add some crumbled feta cheese on top. Brush the edges of the dough with the beaten egg. Fold the dough over the filling, forming a half-moon shape and press the edges to seal.

Place the empanadas on a baking sheet lined with parchment paper. Brush the top with the beaten egg. Bake those bad boys in the oven at 375F (190C) for 15-20 minutes or until golden brown. Serve 'em up nice and warm, maybe with some tzatziki or hummus on the side.

And there you have it folks, the perfect Spinach and Feta Empanadas.

Enjoy

85. Fig and Goat Cheese Empanadas

Prep: 20 min. Cook: 20 min. Ready In: 40 min. Servings: 4

Ingredients:

Store-bought empanada dough (12 discs)

1 cup dried figs, chopped

4 oz goat cheese, crumbled

1/4 cup honey

1/4 cup walnuts, chopped

1 tablespoon fresh rosemary, finely chopped

1/4 teaspoon black pepper

1 egg, beaten (for egg wash)

Cooking Directions:

Indulge in a symphony of sweet and savory flavors with these Fig and Goat Cheese Empanadas. The irresistible combination of succulent figs, creamy goat cheese, and aromatic rosemary creates a culinary masterpiece that will delight your senses. Perfect for a sophisticated appetizer or a decadent dessert, these empanadas are a celebration of indulgence.

In a large mixing bowl, combine the chopped dried figs, crumbled goat cheese, honey, chopped walnuts, fresh rosemary, and black pepper. Mix until the ingredients are evenly distributed.

Preheat your oven to 400°F (200°C) and line a baking sheet with parchment paper. Roll out the store-bought empanada dough and cut out circles about 5 inches in diameter. You can use a round cookie cutter or an appropriately sized bowl as a guide. Place a spoonful of the fig and goat cheese filling in the center of each dough circle.

Fold the dough over the filling, creating a half-moon shape, and press the edges together with your fingers to seal. You can use a fork to create a decorative pattern around the edges if you'd like.

Arrange the filled empanadas on the prepared baking sheet. Brush the tops with the beaten egg to give them a gorgeous golden sheen.

Bake the empanadas for 20 to 25 minutes, or until they're golden brown and crispy. Allow them to cool for a few minutes before serving.

And there you have it – Fig and Goat Cheese Empanadas that are a true delight for the senses. Share these exquisite treats with friends and family as you savor the harmonious blend of flavors or enjoy them on your own as a luxurious escape from the ordinary. One bite, and you'll be transported to a world of culinary enchantment.

Enjoy

86. Apple and Cheddar Empanadas

Prep: 20 min. Cook: 20 min. Ready In: 40 min. Servings: 4

Ingredients:

Store-bought empanada dough (12 discs)

2 cups apples, peeled and diced (about 2 medium-sized apples)

1 cup sharp cheddar cheese, grated

1/4 cup brown sugar

1/4 cup all-purpose flour

1/2 teaspoon ground cinnamon

1/4 teaspoon ground nutmeg

1/4 teaspoon salt

1 egg, beaten (for egg wash)

Cooking Directions:

Savor the sweet and savory goodness of these Apple and Cheddar Empanadas. The delightful combination of juicy apples, sharp cheddar cheese, and warm spices creates a mouthwatering treat that's perfect for any occasion. Whether you serve them as a delicious appetizer or a satisfying dessert, these empanadas are sure to impress.

In a large mixing bowl, combine the diced apples, grated cheddar cheese, brown sugar, all-purpose flour, ground cinnamon, ground nutmeg, and salt. Mix until the ingredients are evenly distributed and the apples are well-coated. Preheat your oven to 400°F (200°C) and line a baking sheet with parchment paper. Roll out the store-bought empanada dough and cut out circles about 5 inches in diameter. You can use a round cookie cutter or an appropriately sized bowl as a guide. Place a spoonful of the apple and cheddar filling in the center of each dough circle. Fold the dough over the filling, creating a half-moon shape, and press the edges together with your fingers to seal. You can use a fork to create a decorative pattern around the edges if you'd like. Arrange the filled empanadas on the prepared baking sheet. Brush the tops with the beaten egg to give them a gorgeous golden sheen. Bake the empanadas for 20 to 25 minutes, or until they're golden brown and crispy. Allow them to cool for a few minutes before serving.

And there you have it – Apple and Cheddar Empanadas that are a delightful blend of sweet and savory flavors. Share these scrumptious treats with friends and family or enjoy them on your own as a delicious escape from the everyday. No matter how you choose to savor them, these empanadas are a celebration of all things delicious and comforting.

Enjoy

87. Egg and Cheese Empanadas

Prep: 20 min. Cook: 30 min. Ready in: 50 min. Servings: 4

Ingredients:

1 package of store-bought empanada dough

4 eggs

1 cup of shredded cheese

Salt and pepper, to taste

1 egg, beaten (for egg wash)

Cooking Directions:

Listen up folks, I got a recipe for you that's going to knock your socks off. These Egg and Cheese Empanadas are the real deal. I'm talking flaky, golden-brown dough with a warm, gooey center of scrambled eggs and melted cheese. And the best part? You can make them in under an hour, using store-bought dough. So, forget about the fancy, fancy. Let's get down and dirty with some empanadas.

First things first, preheat that oven to 375 degrees. Trust me, you don't want to skimp on the heat. Next, scramble some eggs in a skillet, seasoning with salt and pepper to taste. Once they're cooked, let them cool.

Now, take that store-bought dough and roll it out on a floured surface. Cut out circles with a round cutter. Place a spoonful of scrambled eggs and a sprinkle of shredded cheese in the center of each dough circle. Fold the dough over to form a half-moon shape and press the edges to seal. Brush the top of each empanada with beaten egg.

Place the empanadas on a baking sheet and pop them in the oven for 20 minutes, or until golden brown. And there you have it, folks. The perfect snack or meal, ready in under an hour. Serve them up with a cold beer and enjoy the goodness.

Enjoy

88. Egg and Ham Empanadas

Prep: 15 min. Cook: 30 min. Ready In: 45 min. Servings: 4

Ingredients:

All-purpose flour for dusting

1/2-pound cooked ham, diced

1/4 cup diced onion

1/4 cup diced red bell pepper

1/4 cup diced green bell pepper

2 cloves garlic, minced

1/4 cup chopped fresh cilantro leaves

1 tablespoon olive oil

Salt and ground black pepper to taste

1 cup shredded Monterey Jack cheese

4 large eggs, beaten

1 (15 ounce) package empanada dough or store-bought pie crust

Cooking Directions:

You know, I've always been a fan of empanadas. The flaky crust and the savory filling - it's the perfect combination of textures and flavors. And these egg and ham empanadas, well, they're a classic. They're the perfect party food, or even just a casual lunch. So, grab a beer, and let's get to work.

Preheat oven to 375 degrees F (190 degrees C).

In a large skillet, heat olive oil over medium heat. Add onion, red bell pepper, green bell pepper, and garlic. Cook and stir until vegetables are tender. Stir in cilantro. Season with salt and pepper.

Remove skillet from heat. Stir in ham and shredded cheese. Add beaten eggs and mix well.

Roll out empanada dough on a lightly floured surface to about 1/8-inch thickness. Cut into 4-inch circles.

Place a heaping tablespoon of filling on one half of each circle. Fold dough over filling, and press edges to seal. Crimp edges with a fork to ensure a tight seal.

Place empanadas on a baking sheet.

Bake in the preheated oven for 20 to 25 minutes, or until golden brown.

There you have it folks, perfect egg and ham empanadas. These are best served hot, but they're also great at room temperature. So go ahead, grab one, or two, or three. And as always, enjoy your meal.

Enjoy

89. Egg and Chorizo Empanadas

Prep: 20 min. Cook: 20 min. Ready in: 40 min. Servings: 4

Ingredients:

1/2-pound Mexican chorizo, casings removed

1/2 cup diced onion

1/2 cup diced red bell pepper

1/4 cup diced jalapeno pepper

1/4 cup diced poblano pepper

1/4 cup diced green bell pepper

1/2 teaspoon ground cumin

1/2 teaspoon smoked paprika

1/4 teaspoon cayenne pepper

1/4 teaspoon black pepper

1/4 teaspoon salt

4 large eggs

1/4 cup heavy cream

1/4 cup grated cheddar cheese

1/4 cup grated Monterey Jack cheese

1/4 cup grated queso fresco

1 package (15 oz) store-bought empanada dough

1 large egg, beaten with 1 tablespoon water

Cooking Directions:

Alright, listen up folks, this recipe for Egg and Chorizo Empanadas is a game changer.

First things first, preheat your oven to 375 degrees F. Next, heat a skillet over medium-high heat and cook the chorizo until browned, about 5 minutes. Remove the chorizo from the skillet with a slotted spoon and set it aside. Add the onion, red bell pepper, jalapeno pepper, poblano pepper, and green bell pepper to the skillet, and cook until softened, about 5 minutes. Stir in the cumin, smoked paprika, cayenne pepper, black pepper, and salt. Cook for another minute. In a separate bowl, whisk together the eggs and heavy cream. Pour the mixture into the skillet and cook, stirring constantly, until the eggs are set, about 5 minutes. Stir in the chorizo, cheddar cheese, Monterey Jack cheese, and queso fresco. Now it's time to assemble the empanadas. Roll out the empanada dough on a lightly floured surface to about 1/8-inch thickness. Cut the dough into 4-inch circles using a round cookie cutter or the rim of a glass. Spoon about 2 tablespoons of the chorizo and egg filling onto one half of each dough circle, leaving a 1/2-inch border around the edges. Brush the beaten egg around the edges of the dough, then fold the dough over the filling to form a half-moon shape. Press the edges together to seal.

Place the empanadas on a baking sheet and brush the tops with the remaining beaten egg. Bake for 20 minutes, or until golden brown.

Serve hot, garnished with fresh chopped cilantro, or with a spicy salsa on the side. And don't forget a cold beer because these empanadas are going to knock your socks off.

Enjoy

90. Egg and Bacon Empanadas

Prep: 15 min. Cook: 20 min. Ready In: 35 min. Servings: 4

Ingredients:

All-purpose flour for dusting

1 package store-bought empanada dough

4 eggs

4 slices of bacon, cooked and diced

1/4 cup diced onion

1/4 cup diced bell pepper

1/4 cup diced jalapeño pepper

1/4 cup shredded cheddar cheese

Salt and pepper

1 egg, beaten

Cooking Directions:

Empanadas, the ultimate comfort food. And today, we're going to be making something that's going to knock your socks off, Egg and Bacon Empanadas. These bad boys are packed with flavor and perfect for a lazy brunch or a satisfying snack. So, let's get cracking.

Preheat the oven to 375 degrees F (190 degrees C). Line a baking sheet with parchment paper. Dust a clean surface with flour and roll out the empanada dough to 1/8-inch thickness. In a medium skillet, scramble the eggs until cooked through. In a medium bowl, combine the scrambled eggs, bacon, onion, bell pepper, jalapeño pepper, cheddar cheese, salt, and pepper.

Place a heaping tablespoon of the filling onto one half of each round of dough, leaving a 1/2-inch border around the edges.

Brush the edges of the dough with the beaten egg, then fold the dough over the filling and press the edges to seal.

Place the empanadas on the prepared baking sheet and brush the tops with the remaining egg.

Bake for 20 minutes, or until golden brown.

And there you have it folks, Egg and Bacon Empanadas. Perfect for a lazy brunch or a satisfying snack, these babies are sure to please. So, go ahead and give them a try, and let me know what you think. Bon Appetit!

Enjoy

91. Egg and Sausage Empanadas

Prep: 20 min. Cook: 20 min. Ready in: 40 min. Servings: 4

Ingredients:

4 pie crusts

4 eggs

1/2 lb. breakfast sausage, crumbled and cooked

1/4 cup diced onion

1/4 cup diced red bell pepper

1 clove garlic, minced

Salt and pepper to taste

1 egg, beaten

2 tbsp olive oil

Cooking Directions:

Alright folks, it's time to get our brunch on with our next dish! Today, we're making Egg and Sausage Empanadas, a savory and satisfying meal that's perfect for breakfast or brunch. With store-bought pie crust dough and a few simple ingredients, we're going to create a dish that's easy to make and oh-so delicious.

Alright, let's start by preheating our oven to 400°F.

In a pan, we're going to heat up some olive oil over medium heat, and then add in some minced garlic, diced onion, and diced red bell pepper. Cook until those veggies are nice and soft, about 5 minutes.

Next, in a separate pan, we'll scramble our eggs until they're cooked. And then, remove from heat and let it cool.

We're gonna take our store-bought pie crust and cut it into 4 equal pieces. Roll each piece into a circle, about 7-8 inches in diameter.

Spoon some of the crumbled and cooked sausage, eggs, and veggies onto one half of each pie crust circle, leaving about a half inch of space around the edges. Brush the edges with a beaten egg, and then fold the other half of the pie crust over the filling, pressing the edges together to seal.

Place the empanadas on a baking sheet lined with parchment paper, and brush the top of each empanada with the remaining beaten egg.

Pop 'em in the oven and bake for 15-20 minutes, or until the crust is nice and golden brown.

And there you have it, folks! Egg and Sausage Empanadas that are easy to make and loaded with flavor. Perfect for a lazy Sunday brunch or a quick and easy breakfast. Serve with a cup of coffee and you're good to go.

Enjoy

92. Egg and Onion Empanadas

Prep: 30 min. Cook: 20 min. Ready in:50 min. Servings: 4

Ingredients:

4 large eggs, beaten

1/2 cup diced onion

1/2 cup diced red bell pepper

1/2 teaspoon dried thyme

1/2 teaspoon dried basil

1/2 teaspoon salt

1/4 teaspoon black pepper

1 tablespoon olive oil

1 package of empanada dough

1 egg, beaten

Cooking Directions:

Attention foodies, it's time to get your taste buds ready for a breakfast revolution! These Egg and Onion Empanadas are a twist on the classic breakfast dish, with fluffy eggs, savory onions, and sweet red bell peppers tucked inside a flaky, golden crust.

To start, heat the olive oil in a large skillet over medium heat. Add the onion and red bell pepper and cook until soft and translucent, about 5 minutes. Then, pour in the beaten eggs and cook until set, about 5-7 minutes. Stir in the thyme, basil, salt, and pepper. Set aside to cool.

Next, preheat your oven to 375°F and line a baking sheet with parchment paper. Roll out the empanada dough on a lightly floured surface to 1/8-inch thickness. Cut the dough into 4-inch rounds. Spoon about 2 tablespoons of the egg, onion, and red bell pepper filling onto one half of each round, leaving a 1/2-inch border around the edges. Brush the edges with the beaten egg and fold the other half of the dough over the filling, pressing the edges to seal. Place the empanadas on the prepared baking sheet and brush the tops with the remaining egg. Bake the empanadas for 20-25 minutes, or until they're golden brown and crispy.

And there you have it folks, the breakfast revolution, the Egg and Onion Empanadas. Each flaky bite is a morning delight, with fluffy eggs, savory onions, and sweet red bell peppers taking center stage. So go ahead, grab a bite and start your day off on the right foot!

Enjoy

93. Egg and Avocado Empanadas

Prep: 30 min. Cook: 20 min. Ready in: 50 min. Servings: 4

Ingredients:

8 oz cooked shrimp, chopped

8 oz cooked scallops, chopped

1/2 onion, diced

1/4 cup chopped cilantro

1/4 cup diced red pepper

1/4 tsp salt

1/4 tsp cumin

1/4 tsp smoked paprika

1 package of empanada wrappers

1 egg, beaten for egg wash

oil for frying

Cooking Directions:

Get ready for a flavor fiesta! Today, we're bringing together the creamy and rich flavors of eggs and avocado, all wrapped up in a flaky and golden crust. These Egg and Avocado Empanadas are sure to be the star of your next meal.

To start, heat the olive oil in a large skillet over medium heat. Add the onion and cook until soft and translucent, about 5 minutes. Then, add the minced garlic and cook for another minute. Crack in the eggs and cook until they're set, about 5-7 minutes. Stir in the diced avocado, salt, and pepper, and cook for another minute. Set aside to cool.

Next, preheat your oven to 375°F and line a baking sheet with parchment paper. Roll out the empanada dough on a lightly floured surface to 1/8-inch thickness. Cut the dough into 4-inch rounds. Spoon about 2 tablespoons of the egg and avocado filling onto one half of each round, leaving a 1/2-inch border around the edges. Brush the edges with the beaten egg and fold the other half of the dough over the filling, pressing the edges to seal. Place the empanadas on the prepared baking sheet and brush the tops with the remaining egg. Bake the empanadas for 20-25 minutes, or until they're golden brown and crispy. And there you have it, a rich and creamy empanada filled with the flavors of eggs and avocado. Each bite is packed with flavor, making for a truly satisfying experience. So go ahead, grab a bite and enjoy the taste of these delicious empanadas!

<u>Enjoy</u>

94. Bacon and Egg Empanadas

Prep: 20 min. Cook: 20 min. Ready In: 40 min. Servings: 4

Ingredients:

Store-bought empanada dough (12 discs)

6 large eggs, lightly beaten

6 strips bacon, cooked and crumbled

1 cup shredded cheddar cheese

1/4 cup green onions, thinly sliced

1/4 cup milk

1/2 teaspoon salt

1/4 teaspoon black pepper

1 tablespoon butter

1 egg, beaten (for egg wash)

Cooking Directions:

Put a fun twist on a breakfast classic with these scrumptious Bacon and Egg Empanadas. Packed with the irresistible combination of smoky bacon, fluffy eggs, and gooey cheese, these empanadas are perfect for a grab-and-go breakfast, a lazy weekend brunch, or even a tasty snack. They're sure to become a morning favorite!

In a large non-stick skillet, melt the butter over medium heat. In a bowl, whisk together the eggs, milk, salt, and black pepper. Pour the egg mixture into the skillet, and cook, stirring occasionally, until the eggs are just set but still slightly soft. Remove from heat and let them cool. Fold the crumbled bacon, shredded cheddar cheese, and green onions into the cooled scrambled eggs, ensuring that the ingredients are evenly distributed. Preheat your oven to 400°F (200°C) and line a baking sheet with parchment paper. Roll out the store-bought empanada dough and cut out circles about 5 inches in diameter. You can use a round cookie cutter or an appropriately sized bowl as a guide. Place a spoonful of the bacon and egg filling in the center of each dough circle. Fold the dough over the filling, creating a half-moon shape, and press the edges together with your fingers to seal. You can use a fork to create a decorative pattern around the edges if you'd like. Arrange the filled empanadas on the prepared baking sheet. Brush the tops with the beaten egg to give them a gorgeous golden sheen.

Bake the empanadas for 20 to 25 minutes, or until they're golden brown and crispy. Allow them to cool for a few minutes before serving.

Enjoy

95. Sweet Corn and Bacon Empanadas

Prep: 20 min. Cook: 30 min. Ready In: 50 min. Servings: 4

Ingredients:

1 lb. pork shoulder, cut into small cubes

1 onion, diced

3 cloves of garlic, minced

1 cup of diced apricots

1 teaspoon of smoked paprika

1 teaspoon of cumin

1 teaspoon of salt

1/2 teaspoon of black pepper

1/4 cup of slivered almonds

1/4 cup of green olives, sliced

1/4 cup of cilantro, chopped

1 package of store-bought empanada dough

1 egg, beaten

Cooking Directions:

Indulge in the irresistible flavors of these Sweet Corn and Bacon Empanadas. The delightful combination of sweet, tender corn, smoky bacon, and gooey Monterey Jack cheese creates a mouthwatering treat that's perfect for any meal. Whether you serve them as a tasty appetizer or a satisfying main course, these empanadas are sure to impress.

In a large skillet, cook the chopped bacon over medium heat until crispy, about 5 to 7 minutes. Transfer the cooked bacon to a plate lined with paper towels to drain the excess grease. In the same skillet, melt the unsalted butter over medium heat. Add the sweet corn, chopped onion, and chopped bell pepper. Season with salt and black pepper. Cook, stirring occasionally, for about 7 to 10 minutes, or until the vegetables are tender and lightly browned. Add the cooked bacon back to the skillet with the corn mixture, and stir to combine. Remove the skillet from the heat and allow the mixture to cool slightly. Once cooled, stir in the shredded Monterey Jack cheese and chopped fresh cilantro. Preheat your oven to 400°F (200°C) and line a baking sheet with parchment paper.

Roll out the store-bought empanada dough and cut out circles about 5 inches in diameter. You can use a round cookie cutter or an appropriately sized bowl as a guide.

Place a spoonful of the sweet corn and bacon filling in the center of each dough circle.

Fold the dough over the filling, creating a half-moon shape, and press the edges together with your fingers to seal. You can use a fork to create a decorative pattern around the edges if you'd like.

Arrange the filled empanadas on the prepared baking sheet. Brush the tops with the beaten egg to give them a gorgeous golden sheen.

Bake the empanadas for 20 to 25 minutes, or until they're golden brown and crispy. Allow them to cool for a few minutes before serving.

Enjoy

96. Cherry and Almond Empanadas

Prep: 20 min. Cook: 25 min. Ready In: 45 min. Servings: 4

Ingredients:

Store-bought empanada dough (12 discs)

1 1/2 cups fresh or frozen cherries, pitted and halved

1/2 cup granulated sugar

1 tablespoon cornstarch

1/4 teaspoon almond extract

1/3 cup slivered almonds

1 egg, beaten (for egg wash)

Powdered sugar (for dusting)

Cooking Directions:

Delight your senses with these exquisite Cherry and Almond Empanadas. The captivating combination of juicy cherries, fragrant almond extract, and crunchy slivered almonds creates a delightful treat that's perfect for any occasion. Whether you serve them as a delectable dessert or a decadent snack, these empanadas are sure to enchant.

In a medium saucepan, combine the cherries, granulated sugar, cornstarch, and almond extract. Cook over medium heat, stirring occasionally, for about 5 minutes, or until the cherries release their juices and the mixture thickens. Remove from heat and allow the mixture to cool. Preheat your oven to 400°F (200°C) and line a baking sheet with parchment paper. Roll out the store-bought empanada dough and cut out circles about 5 inches in diameter. You can use a round cookie cutter or an appropriately sized bowl as a guide. Place a spoonful of the cherry filling in the center of each dough circle, followed by a sprinkle of slivered almonds.

Fold the dough over the filling, creating a half-moon shape, and press the edges together with your fingers to seal. You can use a fork to create a decorative pattern around the edges if you'd like.

Arrange the filled empanadas on the prepared baking sheet. Brush the tops with the beaten egg to give them a gorgeous golden sheen.

Bake the empanadas for 20 to 25 minutes, or until they're golden brown and crispy. Allow them to cool for a few minutes before serving.

Dust the empanadas with powdered sugar for a sweet and elegant finishing touch.

And there you have it – Cherry and Almond Empanadas that are a delightful fusion of flavors and textures. Share these enchanting treats with friends and family, or savor them on your own as a delicious escape from the everyday. With their irresistible combination of sweet and nutty, these empanadas are a true dessert lover's dream.

Enjoy

97. Roasted Garlic and Brie Empanadas

Prep: 15 min. Cook: 25 min. Ready In: 40 min. Servings: 4

Ingredients:

Store-bought empanada dough (12 discs)

1 head of garlic

1 tablespoon olive oil

8 ounces Brie cheese, rind removed and cut into small pieces

1/4 teaspoon salt

1/4 teaspoon black pepper

1 tablespoon chopped fresh thyme leaves

1 egg, beaten (for egg wash)

Cooking Directions:

Indulge in the sumptuous flavors of these Roasted Garlic and Brie Empanadas. The delectable combination of creamy, melted Brie and sweet, caramelized roasted garlic creates a heavenly treat that's perfect for any sophisticated occasion. Whether you serve them as a refined appetizer or a luxurious main course, these empanadas are sure to enchant.

Preheat oven to 375 degrees F (190 degrees C).

In a large skillet, heat olive oil over medium heat. Add onion, red bell pepper, green bell pepper and garlic. Cook and stir until vegetables are tender. Stir in cilantro. Season with salt and pepper.

Remove skillet from heat. Stir in shrimp and shredded cheese. Add beaten eggs and mix well.

Roll out empanada dough on a lightly floured surface to about 1/8-inch thickness. Cut into 4-inch circles.

Place a heaping tablespoon of filling on one half of each circle. Fold dough over filling, and press edges to seal. Crimp edges with a fork to ensure a tight seal.

Place empanadas on a baking sheet.

Bake in the preheated oven for 20 to 25 minutes, or until golden brown.

And there you have it folks, shrimp and garlic empanadas that are sure to be a hit at any gathering. These are best served hot, but they're also great at room temperature. So go ahead, grab one, or two, or three. And as always, enjoy your meal.

Enjoy

98. Nutella and Banana Empanadas

Prep: 15 min. Cook: 20 min. Ready in: 35 min. Servings: 4

Ingredients:

3/4 cup of Nutella spread

1 banana, mashed

1 tsp of vanilla extract

3/4 package of empanada dough (store-bought or homemade)

3/4 egg, beaten (for egg wash)

Cooking Directions:

Alright folks, listen up. We're going to take a walk on the sweet side with these Nutella and Banana Empanadas, it's a combination of flavors that just can't be beat.

In a bowl, mix Nutella, mashed banana, and vanilla extract.

Next, roll out your empanada dough. I like mine to be about 1/8 inch thick. Cut out some circles. Place a tablespoon of filling on one side of the dough circle. Brush the edges of the dough with the beaten egg. Fold the dough over the filling, forming a half-moon shape and press the edges to seal.

Place the empanadas on a baking sheet lined with parchment paper. Brush the top with the beaten egg. Bake those bad boys in the oven at 375F (190C) for 15-20 minutes or until golden brown. Serve 'em up nice and warm, maybe with some ice cream or whipped cream on the side.

And there you have it folks, the perfect Nutella, and Banana Empanadas.

Enjoy

99. Blackberry and Cream Cheese Empanadas

Prep: 15 min. Cook: 25 min. Ready In: 40 min. Servings: 4

Ingredients:

Store-bought empanada dough (12 discs)

8 oz cream cheese, softened

1/4 cup granulated sugar

1 teaspoon vanilla extract

1 1/2 cups fresh blackberries, halved

1 tablespoon cornstarch

1/4 cup granulated sugar (for the blackberries)

1 egg, beaten (for egg wash)

Cooking Directions:

Indulge in a delightful dessert adventure with these Blackberry and Cream Cheese Empanadas. The heavenly blend of rich cream cheese, sweet, tangy blackberries, and a touch of vanilla creates an exquisite treat that's perfect for any occasion. Whether you serve them as a sumptuous dessert or a decadent snack, these empanadas are sure to captivate.

In a medium bowl, mix the softened cream cheese, 1/4 cup granulated sugar, and vanilla extract. Stir until the ingredients are well combined and the mixture is smooth. In a separate bowl, gently toss the halved blackberries with cornstarch and 1/4 cup granulated sugar. Ensure the blackberries are well coated. Preheat your oven to 400°F (200°C) and line a baking sheet with parchment paper.

Roll out the store-bought empanada dough and cut out circles about 5 inches in diameter. You can use a round cookie cutter or an appropriately sized bowl as a guide. Place a spoonful of the cream cheese mixture in the center of each dough circle, followed by a few blackberry halves. Fold the dough over the filling, creating a half-moon shape, and press the edges together with your fingers to seal. You can use a fork to create a decorative pattern around the edges if you'd like.

Arrange the filled empanadas on the prepared baking sheet. Brush the tops with the beaten egg to give them a gorgeous golden sheen.

Bake the empanadas for 20 to 25 minutes, or until they're golden brown and crispy. Allow them to cool for a few minutes before serving.

And there you have it – Blackberry and Cream Cheese Empanadas that are a delightful fusion of sweet and savory. Share these enchanting treats with friends and family, or savor them on your own as a delicious escape from the everyday. With their irresistible combination of flavors and textures, these empanadas are a true dessert lover's dream.

Enjoy

100. Corn and Poblano Empanadas

Prep: 20 min. Cook: 20 min. Ready in: 40 min. Servings: 4

Ingredients:

Store-bought empanada dough (12 discs)

2 cups corn kernels (fresh, frozen, or canned)

1 large poblano pepper, roasted, peeled, seeded, and chopped

1 small onion, finely chopped

2 cloves garlic, minced

1/2 cup shredded cheese (Monterey Jack or mozzarella)

2 tablespoons olive oil

1/4 teaspoon ground cumin

1/4 teaspoon salt

1/4 teaspoon black pepper

1 egg, beaten (for egg wash)

Cooking Directions:

Get ready to embark on a sensational flavor journey with these Corn and Poblano Empanadas. Each bite bursts with the sweetness of corn and the mild, smoky heat of roasted poblano peppers, all wrapped in a flaky, golden pastry. Perfect for a summer get-together or a comforting snack on a chilly evening, these empanadas will delight your taste buds with their unique and captivating taste.

In a large skillet, heat the olive oil over medium heat. Add the chopped onions and garlic, and sauté until the onions become translucent and the garlic is fragrant, about 3 to 5 minutes. Add the corn kernels and cook for another 5 minutes, stirring occasionally. If you're using frozen corn, cook until the corn is heated through and any excess moisture has evaporated. Stir in the chopped poblano pepper and ground cumin. Cook for another 2 to 3 minutes, allowing the flavors to meld together. Season with salt and pepper, then remove from heat and let the mixture cool. Preheat your oven to 400°F (200°C) and line a baking sheet with parchment paper. Roll out the store-bought empanada dough and cut out circles about 5 inches in diameter. You can use a round cookie cutter or an appropriately sized bowl as a guide. Place a spoonful of the cooled corn and poblano filling in the center of each dough circle, and top it with a sprinkle of shredded cheese. Fold the dough over the filling, creating a half-moon shape, and press the edges together with your fingers to seal. You can use a fork to create a decorative pattern around the edges if you'd like. Arrange the filled empanadas on the prepared baking sheet. Brush the tops with the beaten egg to give them a gorgeous golden sheen. Bake the empanadas for 20 to 25 minutes, or until they're golden brown and crispy. Allow them to cool for a few minutes before serving.

Enjoy

1. Classic Empanada Dough

Ingredients:
2 1/4 cups all-purpose flour
1/2 teaspoon salt
1 stick (1/2 cup) unsalted butter, cold and diced
1 egg
1/4 cup cold water
1 tablespoon white vinegar

Prep Time: 15 minutes
Ready in: 1 hour 15 minutes (includes resting time)

Instructions:
In a large bowl, mix the flour and salt.
Incorporate butter using a pastry blender or fork until mixture is crumbly.
In another bowl, beat the egg, water, and vinegar.
Add wet ingredients to dry ingredients and mix until a dough forms.
Knead briefly, then wrap in plastic wrap and refrigerate for 1 hour.

2. Whole Wheat Empanada Dough

Ingredients:
2 cups whole wheat flour
1/4 cup all-purpose flour
1/2 teaspoon salt
1 stick unsalted butter, cold and diced
1 egg
1/3 cup cold water

Prep Time: 15 minutes
Ready in: 1 hour 15 minutes

Instructions:
Follow the same steps as the Classic Empanada Dough, but substitute with the above ingredients.

3. Gluten-Free Empanada Dough

Ingredients:
2 cups gluten-free flour blend
1 teaspoon xanthan gum (skip if the flour blend includes it)
1/2 teaspoon salt
1 stick unsalted butter, cold and diced
1 egg
1/3 cup cold water

Prep Time: 15 minutes
Ready in: 1 hour 15 minutes

Instructions:
Follow the same steps as the Classic Empanada Dough, but substitute with the above ingredients.

4. Cornmeal Empanada Dough

Ingredients:
1 1/2 cups all-purpose flour
3/4 cup cornmeal
1/2 teaspoon salt
1 stick unsalted butter, cold and diced
1 egg
1/4 cup cold water
1 tablespoon vinegar

Prep Time: 15 minutes
Ready in: 1 hour 15 minutes

Instructions:
Follow the same steps as the Classic Empanada Dough, but substitute with the above ingredients.

5. Herbed Empanada Dough

Ingredients:
2 1/4 cups all-purpose flour
1/2 teaspoon salt
1 stick unsalted butter, cold and diced
1 egg
1/4 cup cold water
1 tablespoon white vinegar
2 tablespoons finely chopped fresh herbs (such as parsley, thyme, or oregano)

Prep Time: 20 minutes
Ready in: 1 hour 20 minutes

Instructions:
Follow the same steps as the Classic Empanada Dough, but add the chopped herbs to the flour and salt mixture before incorporating the butter.

Remember, these doughs can be rolled out and cut into circles for making the empanadas. Once filled, you can bake or fry them according to the recipe's specific instructions.

Thank you for purchasing
Top 100 Most Delicious Empanada Recipes.

We hope you found the recipes as tasteful and delicious as we do.

Please show your support and love for empanadas by leaving a review, if the recipes were delicious.

Make sure to check out all the other delicious recipes in the Top 100 Most Delicious cookbook series.